THE 2023 UK AIR FRYER COOKBOOK FOR BEGINNERS

Delicious, Healthy & Budget-Friendly Recipes
Including Dinners, Sides, Snacks, Lunches & More
(European Measurements & UK Ingredients)

By

Victoria Anderson

Table of Contents

ABOUT THE AUTHOR

A group of Chefs trying to make cooking fun and healthy again!

We know how busy you are, that is why we aim to make our recipes as easy, budget friendly and delicious as possible, so you can cook up meals you look forward to that nourish you simultaneously.

With every book we create we also include a Bonus PDF so you get access to coloured images with every single recipe! We couldn't include them in the book due to printing costs and we wanted to keep the books as affordable as possible. We hope you enjoy!

Please email us & our customer support team will help as soon as we possibly can! We want to make sure you are 100% satisfied and if you have any issues at all please email us and we will do our best to help.

Also, if you have any feedback on how we can improve this book & further books please email us that and we will make all the changes we can. As mentioned we can't add colour photos inside the book due to printing costs, but any other improvements we would love to make!

Our customer support email is **vicandersonpublishing@gmail.com** – as mentioned email us anything you wish here ☺

Happy Cooking!

INTRODUCTION

Food has always been a source of enjoyment for me, whether on a happy occasion or a bad day. It's no secret that what we eat influences our feelings and the world around us. When we eat a balanced diet and get plenty of rest, we have more energy to do things we love doing.

I grew up slim and loved to eat food outside the home, such as chips, doughnuts, chicken strips, and outstanding pre-packaged foods. These foods always came first whenever I thought of eating or dining out. It is important to note that excessive consumption of a fat diet can lead to adverse health risks. Our supermarkets are filled with foods high in saturated fats. It is pertinent to note that overconsumption of these foods may lead to diabetes, heart disease, stroke, and hypertension.

Why do people love to eat fat-filled food? A hearty appetite is enough to satisfy our cravings. Of course, they taste good, crispy, crunchy, and well-cooked. It is okay when one eats it rarely, but it causes a problem if it becomes part of one's lifestyle.

As time passed, I noticed that my weight had increased, and my mind prompted me to make healthier choices and abandon this unhealthy lifestyle. This decision was not initially possible for me, but one day I came across a book that changed my life.

Did you know you can be healthy, get in shape, save your hard-earned money, and enjoy delicious, easy-going food? Does it sound virtuous? Is it an advertorial? No, it is not. It is voracious. You only need to learn the techniques of air frying.

Why are air fryers more popular nowadays? They reduce the amount of fat and oil; 1 gram of fat provides 9 calories, and using an air fryer reduces the number of calories in our meal. It reduces cooking time and thus saves our time for other activities.

One day, I wanted to try this useful kitchen appliance and hoped the result would be satisfying. So, I started with one of my favourite foods, chicken strips. When I took the chicken strips out of the air fryer basket and tried out the first batch, I was pleasantly surprised because it was too good; they came without messy hot pot oil and with far less guilt. I was not going to recline! I was hooked! Food tastes better when we do not feel guilty about eating it.

These air fryers were designed to cook food with minimal fat and high temperature. This is the reason I decided to write this book. This book contains amazing recipes for air fryers that are so luscious that everyone will enjoy them. It contains wonderful recipes for breakfast, snacks, and vegetarian and seafood items, with minimal clean-up.

Healthy options for breakfast and desserts are available to you, and they are accompanied by dishes that will have you salivating in anticipation. As technology increases, many novel products that make cooking easier follow suit. These technological advancements have made it possible for individuals to produce better-tasting meals. It's no secret that air fryers have gained popularity over the last few years.

If you have already purchased and used this device, you will undoubtedly know many ideas and tactics that make your daily meal appetizing. You can't go wrong with an air fryer; it is the best kitchen appliance in decades. Despite its appearance, an air fryer is not a device that will collect dust in your kitchen. It is also used for grilling, baking, steaming, and stir-frying. Yes, you can also bake in addition to healthy meals. So, let's get frying!

AIR FRYER BASICS

The air fryer is a kitchen device that converts air into heat to cook food. It circulates heated air around the food, causing moisture to evaporate and, at the same time, creating a crispy outer crust. It works efficiently when the surrounding air is dry and above room temperature. Moist air causes food to lose its crispiness, steam, and flavour, leading to bland food.

Air fryers cook food faster than conventional baking, boiling, or roasting methods. Because it makes food crispy outside, it is a great choice to bake potatoes and potato side dishes without deep frying them in oil. You can also prepare pizza, fish, doughnuts, nuggets, vegetables, poultry, onion rings, and other dishes in the air fryer. They are already juicy, so they do not need extra cooking oil. In this meal, always remember to use dry seasoning instead of wet seasoning to increase crispiness. If you love barbecue sauce or honey on your meat, apply the glaze at the very end.

To brown and crisp lean meats or other low-fat or fat-free foods, only a small amount of oil is required if cooked in an air fryer. Because of their greater smoking point, canola and vegetable oil are the best choices. And you can use this oil before seasoning pork chops or chicken breasts.

It would help if you first coated them with oil when air frying vegetables like Brussels sprouts, broccoli florets, or potato halves. It is essential to sprinkle some salt before air frying. Some types of air fryers can do baked and toasted. These designs are more reminiscent of older-style ovens. So, you can roast chicken wings or bake brownies. Many air fryers have small baskets that make it difficult to prepare larger meals.

You will be amazed that air fryer food tastes much better than normal cooking methods. The demand for fried food has increased recently; however, everyone wants to maintain their health while consuming something delicious.

Air fryer manufacturers market their products as a way to enjoy deep-fried dishes without worrying about their detrimental effects on the human body because meals cooked using air fryers have less oil than other foods. It is a healthy and good cooking device that requires little-to-no oil.

HOW DOES AN AIR FRYER WORK?

The air fryer uses a simple principle, the same as used in convection ovens. In the air fryer, hot air is released in one direction, and it rises to the upper level. In this case, hot air is circulated inside a sealed container, typically perforated sealed bags or tubes, and heated food is placed inside it. It requires a high-powered fan to circulate superheated air from the top of the cooking chamber. Electricity is needed in heating the appliance.

The hot air prevents contamination of food while it cooks. The air fryer uses a blower fan to pump heated air into the container. The perforated basket of the air fryer aids in better circulation. This heats the food up to an internal temperature of 200°C, which is enough to cook the food quickly and evenly. Such high temperatures require no oil.

Air fryers use superheated air with fine oil droplets to remove moisture from food. Hence, the dish retains the same texture and flavour as its deep-fried counterparts while having a fraction of the fat content.

ARE THERE ANY DIFFERENCES BETWEEN AN AIR FRYER AND AN OVEN?

An air fryer is a miniature oven with a powerful fan that pumps hot air around your favourite foods, such as chicken wings and vegetables. An air fryer differs from an oven because it circulates hot air rather than cooking with heat. The heating element and fan are fixed at the top of an air fryer. Whereas such is not obtainable in an oven.

There are many different modes of cooking, such as convection and non-convection. The non-convection mode helps to cook the food faster, but it also cooks unevenly due to heat fluctuations in the oven, which cause moisture loss.

The convection mode is helpful if you want to cook your food evenly and quickly. In this mode, oil and food are cooked with alternating heat, heated faster in certain areas, and then dropped to a place for cooling. It is a very good method because it maintains proper temperature throughout the device.

There are several different models of air fryers available in the market today. Each has a different amount of internal volume. Larger air fryers are more efficient because they have larger air filters and cook more food at once. Several different models of air fryer do not require preheating time.

Cooking efficiency varies, depending on container size and how often you empty the contents. The models that require preheat time may use more energy. Some models have rotisserie attachments that cook meat, poultry, fish, and other foods with crispy textures and tenderness on the inside. Many models use convection for cooking, which reduces cooking time.

HOW TO CONVERT A RECIPE USED IN THE OVEN TO AN AIR FRYER?

Each oven cooks differently, so some recipes can bake better in an air fryer that does not require much heat. The recipes will do even better at a lower temperature. Place your air fryer basket in the appliance and note how high the basket is positioned. Since most recipes are written for baking in an oven rather than an air fryer, you must take note of the temperature needed. You can check it with a stopwatch or continuously check the food.

Guidelines for Recipe Conversion

- Convert temperature and time.
- Reduce the amount of fat because cooking in an air fryer does not require too much fat. So, you must reduce the amount of fat in an air fryer. Always test the food before serving to check whether there is a need for more oil or not.
- Reduce the time in the air fryer because food in an air fryer does not require as much time as in an oven.
- Food cooked in an air fryer is ready in a few minutes, so check the food to fulfil your requirement.
- If you are using a recipe that needs seasoning and herbs, you are supposed to add them when your food is almost ready; otherwise, you may have burnt food.
- In some recipes, you will need to increase the salt content because an air fryer does not heat as much as an oven so you will lose more natural juice in your food.

FEATURES OF THE AIR FRYER

Air fryers typically have three parts; the air fryer's base, basket base, and basket. The air fryer base is an important part of the air fryer. The basket base is normally positioned at the bottom of the appliance, which retains the basket.

Confectionary crumbs and oil that fall through perforations in the basket's base are to be contained by this base. The food is stored in the basket attached to this device's bottom. Both the basket and base basket are dishwasher safe. Some air fryers include a double grill layer, baking tray, and divider.

The Cooking Chamber: The main body of an air fryer is to hold the food. It consists of a basket or wire rack to support food during cooking oil and a lid to contain the hot air around your food.

The Handle: It is used to take out food without burning one's hands. It is usually covered with a silicone sleeve for added grip and protection.

Temperature Settings: A digital display shows the temperature; this includes the temperature for frying, sautéing, searing, and baking.

The Timer Control Knob: The timer control knob is set for the desired cook times. This is a minor feature.

The Lid: This is on top of the air fryer. It is designed to seal the hot air and keep it circulating in your food.

The Air Inlet: The air inlet is the hole that gets hot air for cooking.

The Air Outlet: The air outlet allows perforated excess hot air to be released from chambers.

BENEFITS OF AN AIR FRYER

An Air Fryer Is Safer than an Oven

It is safer because its inside is coated with a non-stick pan coating, reducing the risk of oil splattering. It has the feature of a cool touch handle and a safety interlock system to prevent it from getting stuck onto the heating element.

Cook from Frozen

It is a great idea to cook frozen food in an air fryer. It cooks food without compromising its nutrients. Always slice your meat into small pieces to avoid the dangers of consuming relatively raw meat.

Healthier

People who follow a diet high in fat are more likely to suffer from heart attacks, diabetes, blood pressure, and cancer. The trans-fat in food increases cholesterol levels, so you should abstain from these foods. By making use of an air fryer, you can prevent these diseases. If you are trying to lose weight, air-fried food is the best option. It is the best method to reduce fat and calorie quantities in your food.

Time- and Money-Saving

An air fryer outperforms a conventional oven for frying food. Using an air fryer saves time because the temperature is set in the air fryer, and it also uses less energy, reducing your utility costs.

Multiple Uses

It can be used for baking, grilling, or reheating food. You may cook an entire chicken at once, depending on the unit size.

FOODS THAT YOU CAN COOK IN AN AIR FRYER AND FOODS TO AVOID

Cakes and Other Baked Foods

Cake and other baked foods generally work well in an air fryer. You can either bake them on wire racks or paper towels. Avoid overlapping the racks when placing them inside an air fryer. Place the cake on the rack closest to the heating element if you plan to bake more items at once, such as cake and cookies. If you want to bake something fragile, like a flan, place it on the rack farther away from the heating element. Remember to check it regularly because it may take less time to cook.

Bagels

Bagels are great items to cook in an air fryer. You have to maintain the temperature of the air fryer when making bagels. It is best to place the racks on top of a baking sheet to catch any drip or spills, then place them in an air fryer and cook at 190°C for 15 minutes. Check it after 10 minutes to ensure its crispiness.

Biscuits

Biscuits cook very well in an air fryer. First, place them in a single layer on top of wire racks. Bake them in the middle of your rack. After 20 minutes, remove them from the rack.

Casseroles

Casseroles are best made in an air fryer. They cook faster than in an oven. Covering the top in aluminium foil is best before placing it into an air fryer. Cook at 190°C for 20 minutes and place it in the refrigerator while preparing the rest of the meal. Refrigerate for 20–30 minutes before baking, transfer it to a rack, and finish baking at 200°C for 20–30 minutes more.

Desserts

Desserts like cake pies, cookies, and brownies bake well in an air fryer. But if you are trying to make pastry and puddings, you have to be careful not to overfill the air fryer, and then you must control and continuously check the temperature. If your air fryer has no temperature setting, try to preheat it. Just remember that it takes less time than the oven.

Fish

Fish is also a great food you can cook in an air fryer. It should be placed on top of wire racks in a single layer and then cooked at 190°C for 20 minutes.

Mushrooms

Mushrooms cook well in an air fryer but tend to become soft and rubbery. So, if you want to cook mushrooms in an air fryer, cook them separately and add them to other dishes. Place the mushrooms on wire racks, leaving at least a 2.5-cm gap between the rack and the mushroom. Cook at 200°C for 20 minutes. Remove the tray, cover it with a towel, and leave them to cool while you cook the rest of your dinner.

The worst foods that are cooked in an air fryer are those that are better suited for a stovetop or slow cooker:

Soups and Sauces

Soups are liquid, so they do not cook well in the air fryer because of their liquid nature. The fast airflow blows very quickly and causes a mess. The same applies to sauces.

Pasta

Cooking pasta and noodles always requires boiling water. This process would be difficult, not only because of the limited space available in an air fryer, but it would be problematic to have to stir the noodles constantly.

Fresh Fruit

Fresh fruit does not work well when cooked in an air fryer. You can use an air fryer for fresh fruit if you wish, except for bananas, which should be left under a closed plastic bag and then cooked at 190°C for 20 minutes. After 20 minutes, you can open it and check whether the food is cooked. If not, leave it in the air fryer for another 15 minutes.

TIPS FOR USING THE AIR FRYER

Do not fill the basket all the way.

This practice is helpful if you want to cook your food evenly and eat it sparingly in the air fryer. This is useful to provide hot air to circulate in the air fryer.

Do not let the oil get too hot.

Always ensure your oil is not too hot when you want to prepare a larger meal. The too-hot oil cannot circulate properly. It will pool at the bottom, coating everything in the basket. It is a good idea to check the oil temperature before placing your food. You may also need to add cold water to reduce the temperature.

Use the right temperature and time.

If you are new to air fryers or if you buy a new model, do not use the temperature and time according to your old model. Always read the instruction manual carefully. The recommended temperature will depend on what you are cooking. If you want to fry products like chicken wings, use a lower temperature because it may prevent the oil from boiling and boiling. Use a thermometer to ensure your food is cooked properly and evenly. Ensure that the temperature is not higher than recommended and that the device beeps when your food is ready to serve. If you do not have a thermometer, it's okay because some air fryers have built-in thermometers to set the temperature and time.

Cook smaller portions.

If you want to prepare a larger batch of food at once, make it in smaller portions; this way, the oil will not circulate and stick to the bottom of the basket every time you cook. Cooking smaller portions are also a sure way to get the best result for your food.

Use a non-stick pan or mat.

A non-stick pan or mat is useful for keeping the air fryer clean. If you do not have a mat, use parchment paper or foil to ensure your food does not stick to the bottom of the basket.

Check the basket frequently.

Constantly checking the basket is the best practice. When cooking something that you want to make crispy, you must turn it in the air fryer halfway through cooking to avoid overcooking and dryness. Chicken wings and asparagus, for instance, may need more oil. You can stir while cooking to ensure the best results.

Clean before and after use.

Always clean your air fryer before every use so there is no build-up after cooking. You can use diluted bleach and scrub it with a sponge. Some fryers come with designed brushes for cleaning. Some models have a removable basket, so you can remove them when you are done.

AIR FRYER SAFETY TIPS

- Always turn off your device when it is not in use. Leaving such an electronic device on may be very harmful while not in use.

- If your air fryer packs up, do not handle it yourself; seek the help of a professional. A warranty may not be accepted if the device is mended by a non-professional. Besides, the problem could be made worse.

- Always follow the temperature stipulated; otherwise, your food may be burnt or overcooked.

- Water and electricity are never compatible. So always dry your hands before operating an air fryer.

- Spray some oil to prevent food sticking to the bottom of the tray.

- Never submerge the appliance in water, as this may cause damage.

Victoria Anderson

BREAKFAST

Don't Forget To Get The Color Images FREE!
Simply Scan The QR Code Below!

Please scan the QR code below to access your bonus PDF with all 150 recipes with full coloured photos & beautiful designs alongside!

This is the only way we can get the recipes with coloured photos to you & keep the book as reasonably priced as possible.

Also, once downloaded you can take the PDF with you digitally wherever you go- meaning you can cook these recipes wherever you may be! (As long as you have an air fryer!)

We hope you enjoy and do let us know your feedback!

STEP BY STEP Guide To Access-

1. *Open Your Phones (Or Any Device You Want The Book On) Back Camera. The Back Camera Is The One You use as if you are taking a picture of someone.*

2. *Simply point your Camera at the QR code and 'tap' the QR code with your finger to focus the camera.*

3. *A link / pop up will appear. Simply tap that (and make sure you have internet connection) and the FREE PDF containing all of the coloured images should appear.*

4. *Now you have access to these FOREVER. Simply 'Bookmark' The tab it opened on, or download the document and take wherever you want.*

5. *Repeat this on any device you want it on! (If you want it on a laptop, simply email the document to yourself!)*

*Any issues please email us at **vicandersonpublishing@gmail.com** and we will be happy to help!!*

SCAN ME

1. FRENCH TOAST STICKS

SERVING: 2; PREP TIME: 10 MINUTES; COOKING TIME: 10 MINUTES
NUTRITIONAL VALUE PER SERVING: 187 KCAL; CARBS: 16G; PROTEIN: 6.7G; FAT: 9G

INGRENKEDIENTS:

- 170g whole wheat bread
- 1 tsp. vanilla extract
- 2 medium-sized eggs
- 2 tsp. cinnamon powder
- 25g brown granulated sugar
- 120 ml milk
- 1 tbsp. melted butter

INSTRUCTIONS:

- Chop each slice of whole wheat bread into three pieces.
- Mix vanilla, butter, and eggs in a large mixing dish and whisk it thoroughly.
- Add sugar and cinnamon to a separate bowl.
- Now dip the breadstick in the egg mixture and sprinkle it with cinnamon and sugar powder.
- Put breadsticks in an air fryer basket and air fry for 10 minutes at 175ºC or until crispy.
- Serve it with maple syrup for a sweet finish.

2. BREAKFAST CASSEROLE

SERVINGS: 4; PREP TIME: 20 MINUTES; COOKING TIME: 15 MINUTES
NUTRITIONAL VALUE PER SERVING: 204 KCAL; CARBS: 13 G; PROTEIN: 15G; FAT: 13G

INGREDIENTS:

- ½ tsp. fennel seed
- 30g turkey breast
- 110g grated cheese
- 30g chopped green bell pepper
- 85g diced onion
- 1 tsp. garlic salt
- 4 eggs, whisked

INSTRUCTIONS:

- Add vegetables to the pan and fry the veggies (onion, bell pepper) and turkey breast until the turkey becomes soft.
- Spray the air fryer basket with oil.
- Place the turkey in the bottom of a small air fryer dish.
- Now sprinkle on the cheese and pour the whisked egg on top of the cheese.
- Pour the garlic salt and fennel seed on top of the egg.
- Air fry for 15 minutes at 190ºC in an air fryer basket.
- Remove the dish from the air fryer and place it on the table to be served.

3. FRENCH TOAST CUPS WITH FRUITS

SERVINGS: 3 PREP TIME: 1 HOUR; COOKING TIME: 15 MINUTES
NUTRITIONAL VALUE PER SERVING: 358 KCAL; CARBS: 48G; PROTEIN: 12G; FAT: 16G

INGRENKEDIENTS:

- 3 medium-sized eggs
- 70g whole wheat bread
- 20 ml maple syrup
- 170g cream cheese
- 95g strawberries
- 185 ml milk

Syrup

- 20 ml maple syrup
- 2 tsp. lemon zest
- 160 ml water
- 375g raspberries
- 2 tsp. corn flour
- 1 tsp. cinnamon
- 2 tbsp. lemon juice

INSTRUCTIONS:

- Glaze the custard cup with oil and cut whole wheat bread into slices. Place half of the sliced bread in the cup.
- Mix the cream cheese and strawberries in a bowl.
- Combine egg, maple syrup, and milk, and pour into a custard cup. Refrigerate for at least 1 hour.
- Now put the remaining bread on top.
- Set the air fryer to 160°C. Heat the custard for 12 minutes in the air fryer until it turns golden brown.
- To make the syrup, combine water and corn flour in a saucepan. Combine the 300g raspberries, syrup, lemon zest, and lemon juice in a mixing bowl.
- Allow them to boil, then reduce to low flame and simmer for at least 3 minutes, or until the sauce has thickened. Mix sauce.
- Place it aside after straining it.
- Pour the remaining berries into the syrup. Enjoy it with a custard cup.

4. BACON AND EGG BREAKFAST BOMBS

SERVING: 2; PREP TIME: 30 MINUTES; COOKING TIME: 10 MINUTES.
NUTRITIONAL VALUE PER SERVING: 190 KCAL; CARBS: 12G; PROTEIN: 8G; FAT: 9G

INGREDIENTS:

- 136g bacon rashers
- 30g butter
- 115g grated cheese
- 4 medium-sized eggs
- 245g buttermilk biscuits
- A pinch of black pepper

INSTRUCTIONS:

- Cut the parchment paper according to the air fryer basket and set it, then spray it with cooking oil.
- Air fry the bacon in a separate pan, until it is crispy. Put it in a paper towel to remove excess liquid and excess fat.
- Butter should be added to the skillet and melted; 4 eggs and black pepper should be whisked.
- Pour the eggs into the skillet and continue to air fry until it is wet.
- Now remove the pan and add the bacon.
- Allow it to air fry for 5 minutes.
- Biscuits should be divided into two layers and covered with at least 1 tbsp. of egg, topped with cheese.
- Place the biscuit in the air fryer.
- Air fry for 4 minutes at 160°C. Air fry more if necessary.

15

5. TEXAS BURRITOS

SERVING: 6; PREP TIME: 20 MINUTES; COOKING TIME: 8 MINUTES
NUTRITIONAL VALUE PER SERVING: 242 KCAL; CARBS: 14G; PROTEIN: 12.5G; FAT: 14G

INGRENKEDIENTS:

- 90g bell peppers, diced
- 170g tortillas
- 60g grated cheese
- 35g cooked sausage
- 170g scrambled eggs
- 1 tsp. of bacon bits

INSTRUCTIONS:

- Combine sausage, cheese, bacon bits, scrambled egg, and bell pepper in a mixer dish and mix it thoroughly.
- Put one-sixth of the mixture in the middle of each tortilla.
- Fold the edges and place them securely.
- Spray the air fryer with cooking oil and air fry at 165°C for 8 minutes.
- Serve and have fun.

6. COURGETTE, ONION, AND BELL PEPPER WITH SAUCE

SERVINGS: 2; PREP TIME: 10 MINUTES; COOKING TIME: 25 MINUTES
NUTRITIONAL VALUE PER SERVING: 180 KCAL; CARBS: 17G; PROTEIN: 2G; FAT: 2G

INGREDIENTS:

- 200g courgettes
- 70g bell pepper (medium-sized)
- 40g red onion
- ½ tsp. olive oil
- ½ tsp. salt
- ½ tsp. black pepper
- 250g marinara sauce
- 1 tsp. chopped basil
- 20g parmesan cheese

INSTRUCTIONS:

- Place the courgettes, bell pepper, and onion in an air fryer tray after cubing them.
- Add oil and spices and mix them with all vegetables thoroughly.
- Put this tray in the air fryer at 200°C for 12 minutes.
- Add marinara sauce to it, and the basil, and put it in the air fryer at 160°C for 3 minutes.
- Top it with cheese and put it again in the air fryer at 200°C for 12 minutes.
- Remove from the air fryer and serve it.

7. SPICED BISCUITS WITH JAM

INGRENKEDIENTS:

- 170g wheat biscuits
- 60g melted butter
- 120g white sugar
- 1 tsp. cinnamon
- 160g fruit jam

INSTRUCTIONS:

- Break the biscuits into two pieces, dip them in butter, and place in the baking pan.
- Air fry at 190°C until they turn brown, usually 3–4 minutes.
- Stir the cinnamon and sugar in a shallow bowl.
- Remove the biscuits from the air fryer and dip them in the sugar mixture while warm.
- Serve with fruit jam.

8. TEX-MEX POTATO HASH

INGREDIENTS:

- 1.4 kg potatoes
- 30 ml olive oil
- 40g red bell pepper
- 10g onion
- 30g jalapeno
- 1 tsp. mix seasoning
- 1 tsp. cumin
- A pinch of salt and black pepper

INSTRUCTIONS:

- Soak potatoes in cool water for 20 minutes.
- Preheat your air fryer to 160°C.
- Drain the water of the potatoes and clean them with a dry towel.
- Drizzle 1 tsp. oil on potatoes and toss to coat.
- Place them into air fryer for 18 minutes.
- Add all other ingredients including the rest of the olive oil and mix.
- Transfer to a potato bowl. Return to the empty air fryer basket and increase the temperature to 180°C.
- Toss vegetables into potatoes and mix evenly.
- Air fry for 6 minutes or until the potatoes become crispy, then cook for another 5 minutes and serve immediately.

9. CHEESY WHOLE WHEAT PASTA WITH SAUSAGE

SERVING: 4; PREP TIME: 5 MINUTES; COOKING TIME: 15 MINUTES
NUTRITIONAL VALUE PER SERVING: 320 KCAL; CARBS: 33G; PROTEINS: 14G; FAT: 12G

INGRENKEDIENTS:

- 560g whole wheat pasta, cooked
- 115g beef or pork sausage
- A pinch of salt and black pepper
- 60g grated cheddar cheese

INSTRUCTIONS:

- Preheat the air fryer to 175°C.
- Place whole wheat pasta and the sausage, cut into chunks, into an air fryer.
- Cook the sausage until piping hot in middle.
- Now put the cheddar cheese on top of the sausage/ pasta and air fry for about 5 minutes or until golden brown.
- Season to taste before serving.

10. OATS PANCAKE

SERVINGS: A 3; PREP TIME: 15 MINUTES; COOKING TIME: 35 MINUTES
NUTRITIONAL VALUE PER SERVING: 167 KCAL; CARBS: 17G; PROTEIN: 5.3G; FAT: 7G

INGREDIENTS:

- 150g oats
- 1 tsp. baking powder
- A pinch of salt
- 1 tsp. granulated sugar
- 1 small egg
- 170g buttermilk
- 1 tbsp. melted unsalted butter

INSTRUCTIONS:

- Add flour, egg, baking powder, sugar, and salt in a mixing bowl.
- Whisk very well and evenly.
- In another bowl add the butter and milk.
- Now mix with other ingredients and rest for 5 minutes.
- Now place in an air fryer, spray with oil and add ½ cup butter.
- Air fry it for 6-8 minutes or until brown.
- Repeat this with all remaining pancakes.

11. MEXICAN CASSEROLE

SERVINGS: 4; PREP TIME: 15 MINUTES; COOKING TIME: 1 HOUR
NUTRITIONAL VALUE PER SERVING: 490 KCAL; CARBS: 26G; PROTEIN: 32G; FAT: 25G

INGRENKEDIENTS:

- 225g minced beef
- 225g sweetcorn and red and green bell pepper mix
- 225g black beans
- 15g onion
- 1 garlic clove, crushed
- 170g Mexican cheese blend
- 225g mini roast potatoes
- 170 ml enchiladas sauce

INSTRUCTIONS:

- Preheat the air fryer to 190ºC and spray a baking dish with cooking oil.
- For 5 to 7 minutes, air fry ground beef or until it turns brown.
- Add other seasonings such as black beans, onion, and sweetcorn with bell peppers.
- Combine the beef mixture in a bowl and add half the cheese, all of the potatoes, and half the sauce.
- Add the mixture to a baking dish and pour on the remaining enchilada sauce.
- Bake for 40 minutes. Sprinkle some cheese and cook until the cheese bubbles.

12. GRANOLA BOWL

SERVINGS: 4; PREP TIME: 5 MINUTES; COOKING TIME: 2 HOURS AND 10 MINUTES
NUTRITIONAL VALUE PER SERVING: 223 KCAL; CARBS: 26G; PROTEIN: 9G; FAT: 8G

INGREDIENTS:

- 80g rolled oats
- 85g toasted wheat germ
- 20g cherries dried
- 1 tsp. cranberries
- 1 tsp. flax seed
- A pinch of ground almonds
- 1 tbsp. honey/maple syrup
- 1 tbsp. olive oil

INSTRUCTIONS:

- Put all dry ingredients into a large bowl and mix well.
- Now spread or spray olive oil onto a baking tray and add all ingredients with the honey/maple syrup.
- Preheat air fryer at 175ºC.
- Bake for 10 minutes or until the granola turns golden brown.
- After removing it from the air fryer, put it in the refrigerator in a cool place for up to 2 hours.

Victoria Anderson

13. APPLE CRISP

SERVINGS: 3; PREP TIME: 5 MINUTES; COOKING TIME: 20 MINUTES
NUTRITIONAL VALUE PER SERVING: 234 KCAL; CARBS: 35G; PROTEIN: 1G; FAT: 9G

INGRENKEDIENTS:

- 445g apple
- 80g brown sugar
- 1 tsp. cinnamon
- 25g whole wheat flour
- 45g butter
- 1 tbsp. lemon juice

INSTRUCTIONS:

- Preheat the air fryer to 175°C. Cut the apple into small cubes, combine it with lemon juice and sugar, and pour it into a tray.
- Cover the tray with aluminium foil and bake for 15 minutes.
- For the topping, mix flour, sugars, and butter in a bowl and spread over the cooked apples.
- Place in your air fryer for 5 minutes.
- Enjoy with cinnamon sprinkled on top.

14. CHERRY TURNOVERS

SERVINGS: 4; PREP TIME: 17 MINUTES; COOKING TIME: 27 MINUTES
NUTRITIONAL VALUE PER SERVING: 290 KCAL; CARBS: 47G; PROTEIN: 4G; FAT: 11G

INGREDIENTS:

- 155g puff pastry sheet
- 240g frozen cherries
- 15g whipping cream
- 90g powdered sugar
- 4 drops of almond extract
- 1 tbsp. pure cane sweetener

INSTRUCTIONS:

- Preheat the air fryer to 175°C.
- Place pure cane sweetener and cherries in a bowl.
- Roll out puff pastry dough and cut it into quarters.
- With the help of a spoon, add the filling to it.
- Fold the pastry and seal the edges (use egg wash if you wish).
- Spray with cooking oil and bake for 25 minutes.
- Remove when they turn golden brown.
- Mix cream, almond extract, and powdered sugar, and drizzle on it.
- Serve and enjoy.

15. SOFT PRETZELS

SERVINGS: 6; PREP TIME: 20 MINUTES; COOKING TIME: 6 MINUTES
NUTRITIONAL VALUE PER SERVING: 152 KCAL; CARBS: 27G; PROTEIN: 4G; FAT: 2G

INGRENKEDIENTS:

- ½ tsp. yeast
- 120 ml warm water
- 120 ml boiling water
- ½ tsp. sugar
- A pinch of salt
- 220g plain flour
- 1 tbsp. butter
- 1 tsp. baking soda

INSTRUCTIONS:

- Combine yeast and warm water in a bowl.
- Combine sugar, salt, and flour in a bowl; add melted butter and knead dough.
- Let the dough rest for 20 minutes; then, make the shape and size of the pretzels.
- Preheat an air fryer to 175°C, then dip the pretzels in boiling water and baking soda and put them in an oil-greased baking tray.
- Air fry each side for at least 3 minutes and then remove it from an air fryer.
- Serve and enjoy.

16. MASHED POTATO TAQUITOS WITH HOT SAUCE

SERVINGS: 2; PREP TIME: 10 MINUTES; COOKING TIME: 30 MINUTES
NUTRITIONAL VALUE PER SERVING: 256 KCAL; CARBS: 40G; PROTEIN: 8G; FAT: 5G

INGREDIENTS:

- 130g potatoes (or ready-cooked mash)
- 1 tsp. milk
- 1 tsp. garlic clove, crushed
- A pinch of cumin
- A sprinkle of minced scallions
- 2 tortillas
- 140 ml red chilli sauce
- 1 diced avocado
- 1 tbsp. fresh coriander

INSTRUCTIONS:

- Preheat the air fryer to 200°C.
- Cube the potatoes, cook them in the air fryer, then mash them when ready.
- Add all spices and milk with the potato in a mixer.
- Run tortillas under plain water and put oil in the frying basket for 1 minute.
- After that, place the mixture in the middle of each tortilla and roll it up on both sides.
- Air fry for 7 minutes or until golden crispy, and serve with chili sauce and avocado.

17. HAM AND EGG TOAST CUPS

SERVINGS: 2; PREP TIME: 10 MINUTES; COOKING TIME: 10 MINUTES
NUTRITIONAL VALUE PER SERVING: 137 KCAL; CARBS: 15 G; PROTEIN: 25G; FAT: 2G

INGRENKEDIENTS:

- 40g crusty bread rolls
- 120g cheese, cut in thin slices
- 2 large eggs
- 1 tbsp. thickened cream
- A pinch of thyme
- 40g Parma ham slice
- 1 tsp. salt and black pepper

INSTRUCTIONS:

- Preheat the air fryer to 165°C.
- Slice off the top of a bread roll, and with the help of a finger, make space for filling.
- Put one cheese slice inside the bread roll. Then one slice of Parma ham.
- Beat the egg into the cream and mix all ingredients together with the spices.
- With a spoon, add the mixture to the roll and put it in an air fryer for 8-10 minutes.
- Serve and enjoy.

SNACKS AND APPETIZERS

**Don't Forget To Get The Color Images FREE!
Simply Scan The QR Code Below!**

Please scan the QR code below to access your bonus PDF with all 150 recipes with full coloured photos & beautiful designs alongside!

This is the only way we can get the recipes with coloured photos to you & keep the book as reasonably priced as possible.

Also, once downloaded you can take the PDF with you digitally wherever you go- meaning you can cook these recipes wherever you may be! (As long as you have an air fryer!)

We hope you enjoy and do let us know your feedback!

STEP BY STEP Guide To Access-

1. *Open Your Phones (Or Any Device You Want The Book On) Back Camera. The Back Camera Is The One You use as if you are taking a picture of someone.*

2. *Simply point your Camera at the QR code and 'tap' the QR code with your finger to focus the camera.*

3. *A link / pop up will appear. Simply tap that (and make sure you have internet connection) and the FREE PDF containing all of the coloured images should appear.*

4. *Now you have access to these FOREVER. Simply 'Bookmark' The tab it opened on, or download the document and take wherever you want.*

5. *Repeat this on any device you want it on! (If you want it on a laptop, simply email the document to yourself!)*

*Any issues please email us at **vicandersonpublishing@gmail.com** and we will be happy to help!!*

1. BEEF TAQUITOS

SERVINGS: 4; PREP TIME: 20 MINUTES; COOKING TIME: 15 MINUTES
NUTRITIONAL VALUE PER SERVING: 247 KCAL; CARBS: 20G; PROTEIN: 16G; FAT: 9.8G

INGRENKEDIENTS:

- 1 large egg
- 80g breadcrumbs
- 225g beef
- 4 tortillas
- 1 tsp. cooking oil
- 1 tbsp. taco seasoning

INSTRUCTIONS:

- Preheat your air fryer to 175°C. Mix taco seasoning, egg, and breadcrumbs in a large bowl.
- Add the beef mixture in it and mix it thoroughly.
- Place the tortilla and add ¼ cup of the mixture in the centre of each tortilla.
- Roll up tightly and fix in place with toothpicks.
- Now, air fry for 6 minutes and flip the taquitos, and air fry for another 6–7 minutes or until brown.
- Serve it with your favourite sauce or dip it like salsa.

2. SPICED CHICKPEAS

SERVINGS: 2; PREP TIME: 5 MINUTES; COOKING TIME: 20 MINUTES
NUTRITIONAL VALUE PER SERVING: 191 KCAL; CARBS: 18G; PROTEIN: 8G; FAT: 6G

INGREDIENTS:

- 210g chickpeas
- 1 tsp. yeast
- 1 tsp. olive oil
- A pinch of smoked paprika
- A pinch of dried garlic
- A pinch of salt
- A pinch of cumin

INSTRUCTIONS:

- Spread chickpeas on a layer of a towel, cover it with another layer of towel, and let it rest for 30 minutes to dry out.
- Preheat the air fryer to 160°C.
- Add all ingredients to a bowl, put in an air fryer-safe dish, and air fry for 20 minutes or until crispy.
- Shake them every 4 minutes for even cooking.
- Serve and enjoy.

3. PASTA AND CHEESE

SERVINGS: 4; PREP TIME: 5 MINUTES; COOKING TIME: 20 MINUTES
NUTRITIONAL VALUE PER SERVING: 152 KCAL; CARBS: 12G; PROTEIN: 7G; FAT: 9G

INGRENKEDIENTS:

- 60g penne pasta
- 1 tsp. olive oil
- 85g cheddar cheese, grated
- A pinch of garlic powder
- A pinch of Italian seasoning
- A pinch of salt

INSTRUCTIONS:

- Place the pot on the stove, add water and salt, and bring it to a boil.
- Add penne pasta, cook for 8 minutes, and drain it.
- Let it rest for 2 minutes.
- Preheat the air fryer at 200°C.
- Put pasta in a bowl and add oil, cheese, seasoning, and salt.
- Air fry for 5 minutes.
- Serve and enjoy.

4. COURGETTE CHIPS

SERVINGS: 8; PREP TIME: 10 MINUTES; COOKING TIME: 12 MINUTES
NUTRITIONAL VALUE PER SERVING: 184 KCAL; CARB: 17G; PROTEIN: 10G; FAT: 8G

INGREDIENTS:

- 240g breadcrumbs
- 150g Parmesan cheese
- 330g courgettes, sliced
- 2 medium-sized eggs
- 1 tsp. cooking oil

INSTRUCTIONS:

- Preheat the air fryer to 175°C.
- Combine breadcrumbs, eggs, and Parmesan cheese in a bowl. Take the courgette slices and dip them into the lightly beaten egg and cheese mixture.
- Arrange the slices into a single layer.
- Air fry it in the air fryer for 10 minutes, flip, and air fry for another 2 minutes.
- Serve and enjoy.

5. AIR-FRIED PUMPKIN SEEDS

SERVINGS: 3; PREP TIME: 20 MINUTES; COOKING TIME: 15 MINUTES
NUTRITIONAL VALUE PER SERVING: 142 KCAL; CARBS: 2G; PROTEIN: 7G; FAT: 12G

INGRENKEDIENTS:

- 70g pumpkin seeds
- 1 tsp. avocado oil
- A pinch of smoked paprika
- A pinch of salt

INSTRUCTIONS:

- Place pumpkin seeds in a small bowl and rinse well.
- Lay two sheets of paper towel on a plate.
- Put pumpkin seeds on it and cover it with a towel.
- Remove water from it and let it rest for 15 minutes.
- Preheat an air fryer to 175°C.
- Put seeds into a bowl and add avocado oil, salt, and paprika.
- Shake the basket every few minutes in the air fryer for 15 minutes.
- Serve and enjoy.

6. BAGEL BITES

SERVINGS: 4; PREP TIME: 20 MINUTES; COOKING TIME: 10 MINUTES
NUTRITIONAL VALUE PER SERVING: 136 KCAL; CARBS: 13G; PROTEIN: 5G; FAT: 6G

INGREDIENTS:

- 60g plain flour
- 1 tsp. baking powder
- 1 tsp. salt
- 120g Greek yoghurt
- 1 egg white
- A pinch of bagel seasoning
- Cooking spray

INSTRUCTIONS:

- Preheat the air fryer to 200°C and spray cooking spray on the basket.
- Whisk flour, baking powder, salt, and yoghurt to mix evenly.
- Knead the dough for about 10 minutes and divide it into quarters.
- Put the dough in the centre of your hand, add cheese, and roll it into a bagel shape.
- Brush the bagel with egg white and sprinkle seasoning on top.
- Put it in the air fryer for 10 minutes or until it turns golden brown.
- Serve and enjoy with your favourite spread.

7. BUFFALO CAULIFLOWER BITES

SERVINGS: 2; PREP TIME: 15 MINUTES; COOKING TIME: 25 MINUTES
NUTRITIONAL VALUE PER SERVING: 125 KCAL; CARBS: 17G; PROTEIN: 5G; FAT: 4G

INGRENKEDIENTS:

- 450g cauliflower, sliced
- 1 tbsp. hot sauce
- 1 egg white
- 40g breadcrumbs
- 20 ml ketchup
- 1 tsp. black pepper
- 2 tsp. red white vinegar
- 1 clove of garlic, crushed

INSTRUCTIONS:

- Whisk egg white, pepper, and ketchup in a bowl.
- Put the breadcrumbs in a mixing bowl.
- Dip the cauliflower slices into this mixture.
- Put this sliced cauliflower into an air fryer and air fry for 25 minutes at 160°C until it turns brown.
- Combine vinegar, black pepper, hot sauce, and garlic in a separate bowl and serve cauliflower with this sauce.

8. AIR-FRIED PICKLES

SERVINGS: 4; PREP TIME: 30 MINUTES; COOKING TIME: 20 MINUTES
NUTRITIONAL VALUE PER SERVING: 26 KCAL; CARBS: 4G; PROTEIN: 1G; FAT: 3G

INGREDIENTS:

- 250g plain flour
- 60g dill pickle juice
- 170g dill pickle slices
- 3 medium-sized eggs
- A pinch of cayenne pepper
- 80g breadcrumbs
- 1 tbsp. fresh powdered dill
- A pinch of garlic powder

INSTRUCTIONS:

- Preheat the air fryer to 220°C.
- Allow all pickles to dry with a towel and let the pickles rest for 15 minutes.
- Combine dill and breadcrumbs in a bowl.
- Combine salt and flour in a mixing dish.
- Combine egg, garlic, and cayenne powder in a separate bowl.
- Coat the pickle in the flour mixture, then in the egg, and then in the breadcrumb mixture.
- Spray the basket with oil and air fry it for 7–10 minutes.
- Flip then continue to air fry for 10 minutes.
- Serve and enjoy.

9. ROASTED SALSA

SERVINGS: 3; PREP TIME: 15 MINUTES; COOKING TIME: 10 MINUTES
NUTRITIONAL VALUE PER SERVING: 30 KCAL; CARBS: 7G; PROTEIN: 2G; FAT: 1G

INGRENKEDIENTS:

- 20g Roma tomatoes
- 25g jalapeno pepper
- 15g red onion
- Cooking spray
- 1 garlic clove
- 60g fresh coriander
- 1 tsp. lime juice
- A pinch of salt

INSTRUCTIONS:

- Preheat your air fryer to 190°C.
- Place tomatoes and jalapeno skin-down into an air fryer basket with the red onion.
- Spray with vegetable oil.
- Air fry it for 5 minutes.
- Open the basket and add the garlic clove.
- Spray with oil and fry for 5 minutes.
- Now cool the vegetables for 10 minutes.
- Remove skin from jalapeno and tomatoes and cut into cubes.
- Put it in the refrigerator for 10 minutes and then serve with coriander and lime juice.

10. TOFU SPRING ROLLS

SERVINGS: 3; PREP TIME: 5 MINUTES; COOKING TIME: 5 MINUTES
NUTRITIONAL VALUE PER SERVING: 101 KCAL; CARBS:14G, PROTEIN: 1G; FAT: 1G

INGREDIENTS:

- 400g tofu
- 50g cucumber
- 30g carrot
- 3 rice paper wrappers
- 30g chilli mango dipping sauce
- Sriracha sauce

INSTRUCTIONS:

- Boil two cups of water on the stove or microwave it.
- Dip the rice paper wrapper into it until it turns pliable.
- Add the cucumber, carrot, tofu cut into strips, and sriracha sauce.
- Preheat the air fryer to 200°C and put the wraps into the air fryer for 5 minutes.
- Serve with chilli mango dipping sauce.

11. ONION RINGS

SERVINGS: 2; PREP TIME: 15 MINUTES; COOKING TIME: 10 MINUTES
NUTRITIONAL VALUE PER SERVING: 311 KCAL; CARBS: 38G; PROTEIN: 12G; FAT: 6G

INGRENKEDIENTS:

- 75g white onion
- 80g breadcrumbs
- 110g buttermilk
- 1 small egg
- 60g plain flour
- A pinch of paprika
- A pinch of garlic powder
- A pinch of salt and black pepper
- Cooking spray

INSTRUCTIONS:

- Spray the air fryer basket with oil.
- Cut onion into slices.
- Add flour to the bowl. Add paprika, garlic powder, salt, and black pepper.
- Add buttermilk and egg into the flour bowl.
- Add breadcrumbs into a separate bowl.
- Dip onion first in the buttermilk mixture and then in breadcrumbs.
- Put it in the fridge for 15 minutes.
- Air fry for 10 minutes at 190°C. Flip if necessary.
- Serve it with sauce of choice.

12. JALAPENO PEPPERS

SERVINGS: 6; PREP TIME: 5 MINUTES; COOKING TIME: 5 MINUTES
NUTRITIONAL VALUE PER SERVING: 219 KCAL; CARBS: 5G; PROTEIN: 6G; FAT: 20G

INGREDIENTS:

- 135g jalapeno peppers
- 1 tsp. oil
- 110g cream cheese
- A pinch of garlic powder
- A pinch of onion powder
- A pinch of salt and black pepper
- 165g cheddar cheese, grated
- 15g cooked bacon
- 2 tsp. chopped chives

INSTRUCTIONS:

- Slice jalapenos and remove seeds from them.
- Rub with oil and put into the air fryer basket.
- Air fry jalapenos at 230°C for 4 minutes.
- Let cool for 5 minutes.
- Place it on a paper towel to drain excess liquid.
- Mix cream cheese, cheddar, bacon, garlic powder, onion powder, salt, and pepper.
- Fill jalapenos with mixture and put it in an air fryer basket.
- Air fry it for 5 minutes and top it with chopped chives before serving.

Victoria Anderson

13. DOUGHNUT HOLES

SERVINGS: 3; PREP TIME: 15 MINUTES; COOKING TIME: 10 MINUTES
NUTRITIONAL VALUE PER SERVING: 110 KCAL; CARBS: 38G; PROTEIN: 16G; FAT: 9G

INGRENKEDIENTS:

- 55g plain flour
- 1 tsp. baking powder
- A pinch of salt
- 225g cottage cheese
- 70g Greek yogurt
- 1 medium-sized egg
- 75g white sugar
- 4 drops of vanilla extract
- A sprinkle of cinnamon

INSTRUCTIONS:

- In a bowl, combine flour, baking powder, and salt.
- In another bowl, add cheese, yoghurt, eggs, sugar, and vanilla extract.
- Mix it evenly with a blender.
- Add wet ingredients to dry ingredients and knead with a hand for 1–2 minutes.
- Preheat the air fryer to 160ºC.
- Coat your palm with oil and roll each dough into a ball.
- Air fry it for about 8–10 minutes.
- Sprinkle cinnamon on while warm.
- Serve and enjoy.

14. CHURROS

SERVINGS: 4; PREP TIME: 10 MINUTES; COOKING TIME: 5 MINUTES
NUTRITIONAL VALUE PER SERVING: 110 KCAL; CARBS: 15G; PROTEIN: 9G; FAT: 28G

INGREDIENTS:

- 60 ml water
- 1 tsp. salt
- 1 tbsp. sugar
- 60g butter
- 60g plain flour
- 2 large eggs
- 1 tbsp. cinnamon

INSTRUCTIONS:

- Mix butter with salt, sugar, and water in a pan and bring it to a boil. Add flour to it. Remove from heat and continue to mix until the smooth dough comes.
- Add eggs one at a time, mix them in, and set mixture aside to cool.
- Preheat your air fryer to 230ºC. Create sticks 7-10 cm long and put them on parchment paper.
- Spray the air fryer with cooking spray and air fry for 5 minutes.
- Roll them in cinnamon sugar and serve.

15. FINGERLING POTATOES WITH DIP

SERVINGS: 4; PREP TIME: 15 MINUTES; COOKING TIME: 20 MINUTES
NUTRITIONAL VALUE PER SERVING: 385 KCAL; CARBS: 36G; PROTEIN: 7G; FAT: 24G

INGRENKEDIENTS:

- 1.2 kg fingerling potatoes
- 25 ml olive oil
- A pinch of garlic powder
- A pinch of paprika
- A pinch of salt and black pepper
- 85g reduced-fat sour cream
- 60 ml mayonnaise
- 25g Parmesan cheese
- 2 tbsp. creamy herb dressing
- 2 tbsp. white vinegar
- 1 tsp. fresh parsley

INSTRUCTIONS:

- Preheat your air fryer to 200°C for 5 minutes.

- Place potatoes in a bowl, add garlic powder, olive oil, paprika, salt, and black pepper, and toss until potatoes are coated; then put them in an air fryer basket.

- Air fry for 15–17 minutes.

- Mix sour cream, cheese, creamy herb dressing, and vinegar to make a sauce.

- Remove from air fry and garnish with parsley and serve with sauce.

VEGETABLE

Don't Forget To Get The Color Images FREE!
Simply Scan The QR Code Below!

Please scan the QR code below to access your bonus PDF with all 150 recipes with full coloured photos & beautiful designs alongside!

This is the only way we can get the recipes with coloured photos to you & keep the book as reasonably priced as possible.

Also, once downloaded you can take the PDF with you digitally wherever you go- meaning you can cook these recipes wherever you may be! (As long as you have an air fryer!)

We hope you enjoy and do let us know your feedback!

STEP BY STEP Guide To Access-

1. *Open Your Phones (Or Any Device You Want The Book On) Back Camera. The Back Camera Is The One You use as if you are taking a picture of someone.*
2. *Simply point your Camera at the QR code and 'tap' the QR code with your finger to focus the camera.*
3. *A link / pop up will appear. Simply tap that (and make sure you have internet connection) and the FREE PDF containing all of the coloured images should appear.*
4. *Now you have access to these FOREVER. Simply 'Bookmark' The tab it opened on, or download the document and take wherever you want.*
5. *Repeat this on any device you want it on! (If you want it on a laptop, simply email the document to yourself!)*

*Any issues please email us at **vicandersonpublishing@gmail.com** and we will be happy to help!!*

1. CRISPY BREADED CAULIFLOWER BITES

SERVINGS: 4; PREP TIME: 10 MINUTES; COOKING TIME: 16 MINUTES
NUTRITIONAL VALUE PER SERVING: 190 KCAL; CARBS: 26G; PROTEIN: 10G; FAT: 5G

INGRENKEDIENTS:

- 45g cauliflower
- 1 tsp. salt and black pepper
- 1 tsp. garlic powder
- 2 large eggs
- 100g breadcrumbs
- 60g Parmesan cheese

INSTRUCTIONS:

- Preheat your air fryer to 200°C for 5 minutes.
- Add cauliflower, salt, black pepper, and garlic powder in a bowl. Then combine evenly; add eggs and mix thoroughly.
- In another bowl, combine breadcrumbs and Parmesan cheese.
- Then dip cauliflower in this mixture.
- Add cooking oil or parchment paper into a baking tray and air fry cauliflower for 8 minutes.
- Flip and spray any dry spots with oil.
- Air fry for 8 minutes until golden crisp or brown.
- Serve and enjoy.

2. BREADED ASPARAGUS CHIPS

SERVINGS: 4; PREP TIME: 10 MINUTES; COOKING TIME: 15 MINUTES
NUTRITIONAL VALUE PER SERVING: 160 KCAL; CARBS: 16G; PROTEIN: 9G; FAT: 7G

INGREDIENTS:

- 455g asparagus
- 1 small egg
- 1 tsp. salt and black pepper
- 1 tsp. garlic powder
- 55g breadcrumbs
- 60g Parmesan cheese
- Oil spray

INSTRUCTIONS:

- Preheat your air fryer to 190°C for 5 minutes.
- Trim the ends of the asparagus.
- Lay them on the board and brush them with egg.
- Season them with salt, pepper, and garlic powder, and gently toss to coat evenly.
- Combine breadcrumbs and Parmesan cheese on a plate and toss asparagus in it.
- Spray all sides with cooking spray.
- Air fry for 5–8 minutes, flip and spray any dry spots, and air fry for another 5 minutes.
- Serve with your favourite dip.

3. BACON-WRAPPED COURGETTE CHIPS

SERVINGS: 4; PREP TIME: 10 MINUTES; COOKING TIME: 15 MINUTES
NUTRITIONAL VALUE PER SERVING: 119 KCAL; CARBS: 9G; PROTEIN: 4G; FAT: 10G

INGRENKEDIENTS:

- 225g courgettes
- 110g bacon rashers
- 1 tbsp. olive oil
- 1 tsp. garlic powder
- 1 tsp. salt and black pepper

INSTRUCTIONS:

- Cut courgettes lengthwise into strips. Spray with oil, and season with salt and pepper.
- Wrap bacon around the courgetti chips and season with salt and black pepper.
- Air fry for 10 to 15 minutes until the bacon is crispy.
- Flip the courgettes, cool for a couple of minutes, and serve.

4. SWEETCORN WITH PARMESAN AND GARLIC

SERVINGS: 6; PREP TIME: 15 MINUTES; COOKING TIME: 18 MINUTES
NUTRITIONAL VALUE PER SERVING: 184 KCAL; CARBS: 19G; PROTEIN: 6G; FAT: 11G

INGREDIENTS:

- 6 fresh sweetcorn cobs
- 60g butter
- 2 tsp. garlic powder
- A pinch of salt and black pepper
- 50g Parmesan cheese
- 60g fresh parsley

INSTRUCTIONS:

- Clean the corn.
- Trim the end of the corn to fit in your air fryer.
- Coat the corn with butter and season with garlic, salt, and black pepper.
- Air fry at 190°C for 10 minutes.
- Flip the corn halfway through.
- Air fry for 3–8 minutes.
- Remove from air fryer, gently coat with Parmesan, and serve warm.

Victoria Anderson

5. ROASTED BRUSSELS SPROUTS

SERVINGS: 8; PREP TIME: 10 MINUTES; COOKING TIME: 15 MINUTES
NUTRITIONAL VALUE PER SERVING: 83 KCAL; CARBS: 10G; PROTEIN: 3G; FAT: 3G

INGRENKEDIENTS:

- 900g Brussels sprouts
- 1 tbsp. olive oil
- 1 tbsp. balsamic vinegar
- A pinch of salt and black pepper

INSTRUCTIONS:

- Add Brussels sprouts to a bowl.
- Drizzle them with oil and balsamic vinegar evenly.
- Season with salt and pepper, and make sure to coat them evenly. There should not be any liquid pooling at the bottom of the bowl.
- Put in an air fryer basket at 180°C for about 10–12 minutes.
- Flip and check halfway through cooking; season with salt and pepper if needed.
- Well-seasoned Brussels are extra tasty. Serve and enjoy.

6. GREEN BEAN CASSEROLE

SERVINGS: 3; PREP TIME: 10 MINUTES; COOKING TIME: 25 MINUTES
NUTRITIONAL VALUE PER SERVING: 235 KCAL; CARBS: 22G; PROTEIN: 9G; FAT: 13G

INGREDIENTS:

- 225g fresh green beans
- 200 ml cream of mushroom soup
- 60 ml milk
- 1 tsp. Worcestershire sauce
- A pinch of garlic powder
- A pinch of salt and black pepper
- 60g fried onions
- 15g cheddar cheese, grated

INSTRUCTIONS:

- Cut green beans into bite-sized pieces. Spray beans with oil, and put them in an air fryer basket.
- Air fry at 170°C for 10 minutes.
- Air fry until green beans are done according to your texture.
- Whisk cream of mushroom soup, milk, Worcestershire sauce, garlic powder, salt, and black pepper in a bowl.
- Pour it over the green beans and gently stir.
- Air fry at 170°C for 11 minutes.
- Air fry until tender and the sauce is bubbly.
- Top it with fried onions and cheese.
- To melt the cheese, fry for 1–2 minutes.
- Serve and enjoy.

7. FRIED AVOCADO TORTILLAS

SERVINGS: 2; PREP TIME: 30 MINUTES; COOKING TIME: 4 MINUTES
NUTRITIONAL VALUE PER SERVING: 203 KCAL; CARBS: 24G; PROTEIN: 4G; FAT: 11G

INGRENKEDIENTS:

- 30g fresh kale
- 1 tbsp. fresh coriander
- 250g Greek yoghurt
- 1 tbsp. lime juice
- 1 tsp. honey
- A pinch of salt and black pepper
- 1 small egg
- 20g corn flour
- 1 tsp. garlic powder
- 2 ripe avocados
- 2 tortillas

INSTRUCTIONS:

- Combine kale, coriander, yoghurt, honey, and lime juice, and put it in the refrigerator overnight.
- Preheat your air fryer to 200°C.
- Then put the egg in a shallow bowl.
- In another bowl, mix corn flour, salt, and garlic powder.
- Dip avocado slices in egg, then into the corn flour mixture, gently patting to adhere.
- Put in a basket and air fry for 3-4 minutes until they turn golden brown.
- Serve avocados with tortillas and the kale/yoghurt mixture.

8. SWEET POTATO ROLLS

SERVINGS: 3 ROLLS; PREP TIME: 10 MINUTES; COOKING TIME: 14 MINUTES
NUTRITIONAL VALUE PER SERVING: 117 KCAL; CARBS: 25G; PROTEIN: 3G; FAT: 1G

INGREDIENTS:

- 120g cooked sweet potato
- 120g self-raising flour
- Cooking oil

INSTRUCTIONS:

- In a bowl, combine sweet potato and flour. Stir with a fork until a dough ball forms.
- Knead the soft dough for about 1 minute.
- Cut into three equal pieces. Allow the dough to rest for 30 minutes to rise.
- Spray the basket with oil.
- Air fry at 165°C for 10–14 minutes.
- Allow it to cool and serve with a sauce of your choice.

Victoria Anderson

9. SCALLOPED POTATOES

SERVINGS: 2; PREP TIME: 15 MINUTES; COOKING TIME: 40 MINUTES
NUTRITIONAL VALUE PER SERVING: 378 KCAL; CARBS: 30G; PROTEIN: 9G; FAT: 25G

INGRENKEDIENTS:

- 240g potatoes
- Oil spray
- 90 ml thickened cream
- A pinch of salt and black pepper
- A pinch of garlic powder
- 30g grated cheddar cheese

INSTRUCTIONS:

- Peel and slice potatoes thinly and spray oil evenly over the potatoes.
- Spray with oil and air fry at 180°C for 18 minutes.
- Combine cream, salt, garlic powder, and black pepper. Stir well until combined.
- Air fry for 18 minutes and pour cream mixture over potatoes.
- Air fry potatoes with the cream mixture at a reduced temperature of 150°C for 15–18 minutes.
- Sprinkle cheese over the potatoes and air fry for 2 minutes until the cheese is melted.
- Allow it to cool for 10 minutes before serving.

10. STUFFED SWEET POTATOES

SERVINGS: 2; PREP TIME: 20 MINUTES; COOKING TIME: 50 MINUTES
NUTRITIONAL VALUE PER SERVING: 376 KCAL; CARBS: 10G; PROTEIN: 12G; FAT: 10G

INGREDIENTS:

- 4 sweet potatoes
- 1 tsp. olive oil
- 1 tbsp. spinach, chopped
- 120g cheddar cheese, grated
- 30g bacon rashers or bacon bits
- 60g chives
- 1 tbsp. cranberries
- 1 ½ tbsp. chopped pecans
- 15g butter
- A pinch of salt and black pepper

INSTRUCTIONS:

- Preheat your air fryer to 200°C. Brush potatoes with oil.
- Air fry for 30 minutes until potatoes are tender.
- Cut in half lengthwise. Scoop out some potato to make a hole for the filling.
- Mash potato, cheese, bacon, onion, cranberries, pecans, butter, salt, and pepper in a clean bowl.
- Reduce heat to 180°C, place filling into potato halves, and air fry for 10 minutes.
- Serve and enjoy.

VEGETARIAN AND VEGAN

Don't Forget To Get The Color Images FREE!
Simply Scan The QR Code Below!

Please scan the QR code below to access your bonus PDF with all 150 recipes with full coloured photos & beautiful designs alongside!

This is the only way we can get the recipes with coloured photos to you & keep the book as reasonably priced as possible.

Also, once downloaded you can take the PDF with you digitally wherever you go- meaning you can cook these recipes wherever you may be! (As long as you have an air fryer!)

We hope you enjoy and do let us know your feedback!

STEP BY STEP Guide To Access-

1. *Open Your Phones (Or Any Device You Want The Book On) Back Camera. The Back Camera Is The One You use as if you are taking a picture of someone.*

2. *Simply point your Camera at the QR code and 'tap' the QR code with your finger to focus the camera.*

3. *A link / pop up will appear. Simply tap that (and make sure you have internet connection) and the FREE PDF containing all of the coloured images should appear.*

4. *Now you have access to these FOREVER. Simply 'Bookmark' The tab it opened on, or download the document and take wherever you want.*

5. *Repeat this on any device you want it on! (If you want it on a laptop, simply email the document to yourself!)*

*Any issues please email us at **vicandersonpublishing@gmail.com** and we will be happy to help!!*

1. OKRA CHIPS

SERVINGS: 8; PREP TIME: 10 MINUTES; COOKING TIME: 20 MINUTES
NUTRITIONAL VALUE PER SERVING: 191 KCAL; CARBS: 37G; PROTEIN: 6G; FAT: 2G

INGRENKEDIENTS:

- 2 large eggs
- 900g okra
- 225g corn flour
- 60g plain flour
- Cooking spray
- A pinch of salt

INSTRUCTIONS:

- Put the eggs in a shallow dish and beat. Gently stir in okra.
- Combine corn flour and plain flour in a plastic bag. Drop the okra in this mixture and shake; remove okra and put on a plate.
- Preheat the air fryer to 200°C. Place breaded okra in a tray and air fry for 4 minutes.
- Shake the basket, mix it with air frying oil, and air fry for at least 4 minutes.
- Air fry for an additional 4 minutes and shake the basket. Air fry for another minute and remove.
- Serve and enjoy.

2. GRILLED PEACHES

SERVINGS: 4; PREP TIME: 5 MINUTES; COOKING TIME: 10 MINUTES
NUTRITIONAL VALUE PER SERVING: 378 KCAL; CARBS: 40G; PROTEIN: 3G; FAT: 24G

INGREDIENTS:

- 4 peaches
- 60g cracker crumbs
- 100g brown sugar
- 115g butter
- Whipped cream

INSTRUCTIONS:

- Cut peaches into wedges and pull out stones.
- In the air fryer, set a piece of parchment paper on top of the rack. Put wedges on it, skin side on parchment paper.
- Air fry at 175°C for 5 minutes.
- Mix crumbs, brown sugar, and butter; flip peaches skin down.
- Spoon crumb mixture over it.
- Air fry for 5 minutes. Using a big spoon, spoon up peaches onto a plate.
- Top with whipped cream.
- Serve and enjoy.

3. SPANISH SPICY POTATOES

SERVINGS: 4; PREP TIME: 4 MINUTES; COOKING TIME: 23 MINUTES
NUTRITIONAL VALUE PER SERVING: 38 KCAL; CARBS: 9G; PROTEIN: 14G; FAT: 9G

INGRENKEDIENTS:

- 4 potatoes
- 30 ml olive oil
- 1 tbsp. chilli paprika
- 1 tbsp. garlic powder
- 20g diced white onion
- 240 ml tomato sauce
- 2 tbsp. red wine vinegar
- 2 tsp. oregano
- 2 tsp. thyme
- 2 tsp. rosemary

INSTRUCTIONS:

- Chop potatoes into wedges and put them in a bowl with olive oil.
- Mix them well and put them in the air fryer.
- Air fry at 160°C for 20 minutes. Shake and air fry for 3 minutes at 200°C.
- Mix all ingredients leftover to make the sauce and serve it with the potatoes.

4. CRISPY CHICKPEAS

SERVINGS: 4; PREP TIME: 10 MINUTES; COOKING TIME: 55 MINUTES
NUTRITIONAL VALUE PER SERVING: 218 KCAL; CARBS: 32G; PROTEIN: 10G; FAT: 6G

INGREDIENTS:

- 225g chickpeas
- 1 tbsp. olive oil
- A pinch of salt and black pepper
- A pinch of paprika
- A pinch of garlic powder
- A pinch of cumin

INSTRUCTIONS:

- Preheat your air fryer to 200°C. Rinse and dry chickpeas with a paper towel.
- Toss chickpeas with olive oil and all the spices in a large bowl.
- Spread chickpeas onto a parchment-lined baking sheet.
- Air fry for 10 minutes or until golden brown.
- Allow them to cool for an hour before serving.

5. VEGETARIAN WONTONS

SERVINGS: 12; PREP TIME: 25 MINUTES; COOKING TIME: 15 MINUTES
NUTRITIONAL VALUE PER SERVING: 141 KCAL; CARBS: 22G; PROTEIN: 4G; FAT: 4G

INGRENKEDIENTS:

- 90 ml vegetable oil
- 360g cabbage
- 360g carrots
- 180g white onion
- 1 tbsp. soy sauce
- 12 wonton wrappers
- 120 ml water
- Cooking spray

INSTRUCTIONS:

- Heat vegetable oil in a skillet over medium-high heat. Add cabbage, onion, carrots, and air fry for 3–4 minutes.
- Remove the skillet and add soy sauce to the cabbage mixture. Cool for 10 minutes.
- Preheat your air fryer to 160°C. Take one spoonful of the cabbage mixture and put it in the wonton wrapper. Seal into a wonton shape.
- Spray with cooking spray and put in the air fryer basket.
- Air fry for 5 minutes, flip, and air fry until golden brown.

6. AIR-FRIED BOW TIE PASTA

SERVINGS: 3; PREP TIME: 10 MINUTES; COOKING TIME: 25 MINUTES
NUTRITIONAL VALUE PER SERVING: 235 KCAL; CARBS: 22G; PROTEIN: 9G; FAT: 13G

INGREDIENTS:

- 450g bow tie pasta
- 1 tbsp. salt
- 2 tbsp. oil
- 2 tbsp. herb seasoning
- 2 tsp. garlic powder
- 1 tsp. chopped chives

INSTRUCTIONS:

- Pour water and salt into stainless steel pot and bring to a rolling boil.
- Add pasta and salt to boiling water and stir. Remove from heat when cooked.
- Preheat air fryer to 200°C.
- Drain pasta (no need to rinse) and coat with spices and oil. Put it in the air fryer basket.
- Air fry for 10 minutes.
- Transfer to parchment paper and allow it to cool.
- Serve and enjoy.

7. FTEMPEH

SERVINGS: 6; PREP TIME: 15 MINUTES; COOKING TIME: 14 MINUTES
NUTRITIONAL VALUE: 389 KCAL; CARBS: 44G; PROTEIN: 16G; FAT: 18G

INGRENKEDIENTS:

- 55g tempeh
- 285 ml BBQ sauce
- 60 ml olive oil
- 1 tsp. sesame seeds

INSTRUCTIONS:

- Cut tempeh in strips. Then, steam it before air frying it because of its bitter taste.
- Preheat your air fryer to 190°C, and brush tempeh with olive oil.
- Air fry for 7 minutes and flip them. Air fry for another 4 minutes. Add BBQ sauce and air fry for 3 minutes.
- When it's done, brush with extra BBQ sauce. Serve and enjoy it.

8. FALAFEL

SERVINGS: 8; PREP TIME: 10 MINUTES; COOKING TIME: 15 MINUTES
NUTRITIONAL VALUE PER SERVING: 91 KCAL; CARBS: 31G; PROTEIN: 4G; FAT: 3G

INGREDIENTS:

- 165g dried chickpeas
- 60g red onion
- 2 tbsp. garlic powder
- 60g parsley
- 60g herb seasoning
- 1 tsp. red chilli flakes
- 1 tbsp. sesame seeds
- 1 tsp. baking powder

INSTRUCTIONS:

- Place dried chickpeas in a large bowl. Soak overnight and then put on a paper towel.
- Add all spices and chickpeas to a blender. Cover the mixture with a lid or plastic wrap and refrigerate for at least 1 hour.
- When ready to air fry, stir sesame seeds and baking powder into the mixture.
- Wet your hands, scoop the mixture, and form it into falafel balls.
- Spray the basket with cooking spray.
- Air fry at 190°C for 15 minutes.
- Serve with pitta bread and salad if you wish.

Victoria Anderson

9. CAULIFLOWER WINGS

SERVINGS: 4; PREP TIME: 15 MINUTES; COOKING TIME: 15 MINUTES
NUTRITIONAL VALUE PER SERVING: 287 KCAL; CARBS: 41G; PROTEIN: 11G; FAT: 9G

INGRENKEDIENTS:

- 250g cauliflower florets
- 120g plain flour
- 1 tsp. herb seasoning
- 240 ml plant-based milk
- 300 ml teriyaki sauce
- A pinch of chili (optional)
- Cooking spray

INSTRUCTIONS:

- Preheat your air fryer to 200°C. Combine all seasoning and flour in a bowl and add gradually the plant-based milk to make a thick batter.
- Rinse and dry cauliflower; dip each piece into the batter, coating completely.
- Put the cauliflower on a tray in an air fryer basket for 10 minutes until it turns golden brown.
- Dip each piece into teriyaki sauce and air fry for another 3–5 minutes.
- Serve warm.

10. LENTIL BALLS

SERVINGS: 4; PREP TIME: 12 MINUTES; COOKING TIME: 12 MINUTES
NUTRITIONAL VALUE PER SERVING: 158 KCAL; CARBS: 18G; PROTEIN: 7G FAT: 7G

INGREDIENTS:

- 100g lentils
- 235 ml water
- 20g croutons
- 1 tsp. olive oil
- 60 ml almond milk
- A pinch of salt and pepper

INSTRUCTIONS:

- Boil lentils in water and cool for at least 10 minutes.
- Add lentils and croutons in a blender and combine. Then add olive oil, almond milk, salt, and pepper, and combine evenly.
- Roll dough into even-sized balls.
- Preheat the air fryer to 175°C, and spray with cooking oil. Air fry for 8–10 minutes.
- Serve and enjoy.

BEEF, LAMB, AND PORK

Don't Forget To Get The Color Images FREE!
Simply Scan The QR Code Below!

Please scan the QR code below to access your bonus PDF with all 150 recipes with full coloured photos & beautiful designs alongside!

This is the only way we can get the recipes with coloured photos to you & keep the book as reasonably priced as possible.

Also, once downloaded you can take the PDF with you digitally wherever you go- meaning you can cook these recipes wherever you may be! (As long as you have an air fryer!)

We hope you enjoy and do let us know your feedback!

STEP BY STEP Guide To Access-

1. *Open Your Phones (Or Any Device You Want The Book On) Back Camera. The Back Camera Is The One You use as if you are taking a picture of someone.*

2. *Simply point your Camera at the QR code and 'tap' the QR code with your finger to focus the camera.*

3. *A link / pop up will appear. Simply tap that (and make sure you have internet connection) and the FREE PDF containing all of the coloured images should appear.*

4. *Now you have access to these FOREVER. Simply 'Bookmark' The tab it opened on, or download the document and take wherever you want.*

5. *Repeat this on any device you want it on! (If you want it on a laptop, simply email the document to yourself!)*

*Any issues please email us at **vicandersonpublishing@gmail.com** and we will be happy to help!!*

1. BAKED BEEF PIE

SERVINGS: 2; PREP TIME: 15 MINUTES; COOKING TIME: 25 MINUTES
NUTRITIONAL VALUE PER SERVING: 212 KCAL; CARBS: 15G; PROTEIN: 12G; FAT: 11G

INGRENKEDIENTS:

* 200g salsa, chunky thick
* 60g cheddar cheese, grated
* 250g ground beef lean
* 225g biscuit crumbs
* 1 white onion, diced
* 100 ml milk

INSTRUCTIONS:

* Preheat your air fryer to 175°C. Spray cooking oil into the pan.
* Air fry beef until it turns brown; drain before stirring in salsa, then spread in pan.
* Stir the biscuit crumbs, cheese, onion, and milk to form a dough.
* Smooth this dough on top of the cooked beef in the pan.
* Air fry for 25 minutes and serve.

2. BEEF FILLET WITH GARLIC MAYO

SERVINGS: 2; PREP TIME: 10 MINUTES; COOKING TIME: 40 MINUTES
NUTRITIONAL VALUE PER SERVING: 400 KCAL; CARBS: 26G; PROTEIN: 19G; FAT: 12G

INGREDIENTS:

* 115g mayonnaise
* 75g sour cream
* 2 tsp. chopped tarragon
* 1 garlic clove
* 1 tbsp. chopped chives
* 75g beef fillet
* 2 tbsp. Dijon mustard
* A pinch of salt and black pepper

INSTRUCTIONS:

* Preheat your air fryer to 190°C. Season beef using salt and pepper.
* Transfer to the air fryer and air fry for 20 minutes.
* In a bowl, mix tarragon and mustard, toss it into the beef, and air fry for 20 minutes.
* Mix garlic, sour cream, tarragon, mayo, and chives separately.
* Serve with this herby mayo dip sauce.

3. BREADED BEEF

SERVINGS: 4; PREP TIME: 10 MINUTES; COOKING TIME: 17 MINUTES
NUTRITIONAL VALUE PER SERVING: 256 KCAL; CARBS: 12G; PROTEIN: 15G; FAT: 5G

INGRENKEDIENTS:

- 3 medium-sized eggs
- 60 ml olive oil
- 500g beef, sliced into 4 pieces
- 1.2 kg breadcrumbs

INSTRUCTIONS:

- Preheat your air fryer to grilling mode. Adjust the temperature to 175°C for 5 minutes.
- Whisk eggs and oil in a bowl. Then breadcrumbs in another bowl.
- Dip each slice of beef in egg mixture and coat with breadcrumbs.
- Arrange on an air fryer plate and grill for 12 minutes.
- Serve and enjoy.

4. MUSTARD MARINATED BEEF

SERVINGS: 2; PREP TIME: 10 MINUTES; COOKING TIME: 45 MINUTES
NUTRITIONAL VALUE PER SERVING: 350 KCAL; CARBS: 27G; PROTEIN: 29G; FAT: 9G

INGREDIENTS:

- 1 tsp. horseradish
- 1 tsp. mustard
- 425 ml beef stock
- 15g butter
- 1 tbsp. fresh garlic, crushed
- 900g beef
- 90 ml red wine
- 85g bacon rashers

INSTRUCTIONS:

- Preheat your air fryer to 200°C. Add horseradish, mustard, butter, and garlic to a bowl. Rub the beef with this mixture.
- Wrap bacon rashers around the beef.
- Cook until beef is to your liking and bacon is crispy.
- Add stock and wine to the pan and lower the temperature to 180°C.
- Air fry for 15 minutes.
- Serve and enjoy.

5. STEAK FAJITAS

SERVINGS: 3; PREP TIME: 15 MINUTES; COOKING TIME: 10 MINUTES
NUTRITIONAL VALUE PER SERVING: 309 KCAL; CARBS: 13G; PROTEIN: 20G; FAT: 7G

INGRENKEDIENTS:

- 400g beef flank, sliced
- 1 white onion, diced
- 1 tbsp. chilli paprika
- 2 tbsp. fresh coriander
- 1 tsp. ground cumin
- A pinch of salt
- 80g fresh tomatoes
- 1 red onion, diced
- 4 tortillas
- 60 ml lime juice

INSTRUCTIONS:

- Combine jalapeno, coriander, cumin, and salt in a bowl. Preheat the air fryer to 200°C. Add seasoning to the beef.
- Air fry for 6 minutes per side until the desired doneness.
- Remove from an air fryer basket and set aside for 4 minutes.
- Put the onion in an air fryer basket and air fry until tender.
- Add the onion and a piece of beef into a tortilla, garnishing with tomatoes and lime juice. Roll up each tortilla into a fajita. Enjoy.

6. CHEESY RIB EYE STEAK

SERVINGS: 2; PREP TIME: 5 MINUTES; COOKING TIME: 10 MINUTES
NUTRITIONAL VALUE PER SERVING: 323 KCAL; CARBS: 1G; PROTEIN: 23G; FAT: 26G

INGREDIENTS:

- 450g rib eye steak
- 1 tsp. olive oil
- A pinch of salt and pepper
- 15g unsalted butter
- 10g blue cheese crumbled

INSTRUCTIONS:

- Microwave unsalted butter and blue cheese crumbled for 30 seconds and stirred it well.
- Refrigerate it while cooking steak.
- Coat steak with olive oil and add your seasoning.
- Preheat your air fryer to 200°C, then Air fry for 6–8 minutes.
- Let it cool for 5 to 10 minutes before serving, and then add the butter/cheese topping.
- Serve and enjoy.

7. STEAK KEBABS

SERVINGS: 2; PREP TIME: 5 MINUTES; COOKING TIME: 14 MINUTES
NUTRITIONAL VALUE PER SERVING: 179 KCAL; CARBS: 6G; PROTEIN; 16G; FAT: 10G

INGRENKEDIENTS:

- 210g beef steak
- 25g red and green bell pepper
- 20g white onion
- 1 tbsp. olive oil
- 100 ml soy sauce

INSTRUCTIONS:

- Preheat your air fryer to 200°C, and spray a basket with oil.
- Cut the steak into cube-sized bites and dip it in the soy sauce. Also, cut bell peppers and onion into bite-sized pieces.
- Take a skewer and add steak, onion, and bell pepper, in that order, and repeat until skewer is full.
- Put this skewer in an air fryer and air fry for 10 minutes.
- Flip and air fry for another 4 minutes.
- Serve and enjoy.

8. MONGOLIAN BEEF

SERVINGS: 6; PREP TIME: 20 MINUTES; COOKING TIME: 20 MINUTES
NUTRITIONAL VALUE PER SERVING: 554 KCAL; CARBS: 57G; PROTEIN: 44G; FAT: 16G

INGREDIENTS:

- 900g flank beef steak
- 80g corn flour
- 1 tsp. olive oil
- A pinch of ginger powder
- 1 tsp. garlic powder
- 130 ml soy sauce
- 135g brown sugar

INSTRUCTIONS:

- Thinly slice the steak and coat in corn flour.
- Place in an air fryer basket coated with oil. Air fry at 200°C for 5–10 minutes on each side.
- While the steak cooks, warm up all sauce ingredients in a medium-sized saucepan on medium-high heat.
- Serve the steak with the sauce.

9. KOREAN BBQ BEEF

SERVINGS: 3; PREP TIME: 15 MINUTES; COOKING TIME: 30 MINUTES
NUTRITIONAL VALUE PER SERVING: 487 KCAL; CARBS: 32G; PROTEIN: 39G; FAT: 22G

INGRENKEDIENTS:

- 225g flank beef steak
- 2 tbsp. corn flour
- Coconut spray
- 2 tbsp. soy sauce
- 50g brown sugar
- 1 tbsp. white vinegar
- 1 clove garlic
- 1 tsp. hot chili sauce
- 1 tsp. ginger powder
- A sprinkle of sesame seeds
- 2 tsp. water

INSTRUCTIONS:

- Thinly slice the steak and toss in the corn flour (save 1 tsp. corn flour for the sauce).
- Add coconut oil to an air fryer basket.
- Add steak and air fry for 10 minutes at 190°C.
- Add sauce ingredients in a pan. Whisk remaining corn flour in boiling water on a hob and then add in the sauce ingredients.
- Remove steak from an air fryer and then add sauce to it.
- Serve.

10. ONION SOUP MIX BURGER

SERVINGS: 2; PREP TIME: 5 MINUTES; COOKING TIME: 12 MINUTES
NUTRITIONAL VALUE PER SERVING: 486 KCAL; CARBS: 18G; PROTEIN: 41G; FAT: 27G

INGREDIENTS:

- 225g minced beef
- 80g onion soup mix
- 2 hamburger buns
- 60g sliced cheese
- 2 fresh tomatoes
- A few leaves of lettuce
- 1 tbsp. mustard sauce
- 1 tbsp. ketchup

INSTRUCTIONS:

- In a large bowl, add minced beef and onion soup mix and make two patties.
- Use foil, spray with oil, and place the patty in it.
- Then air fry for 5–7 minutes.
- Air fry on the other side for 5 minutes at 190°C.
- Serve it in the burger bun with slices of cheese, tomato, and lettuce. Splash on a little mustard and ketchup. Enjoy.

11. BEEF ROAST

SERVINGS: 3; PREP TIME: 15 MINUTES; COOKING TIME: 1 HOUR
NUTRITIONAL VALUE PER SERVING: 620 KCAL; CARBS: 3G; PROTEIN: 26G; FAT: 43G

INGRENKEDIENTS:

- 680g beef roast
- 1 tsp. steak seasoning
- 60g gluten-free gravy mix
- 2 tbsp. water
- 30g unsalted butter
- 1 tsp. fresh parsley

INSTRUCTIONS:

- Preheat your air fryer to 190°C for 5 minutes. Add seasoning to the roast.
- Combine gravy with ½ cup of water and set aside.
- Now, prepare a sheet of foil for the beef to rest on.
- Roll the foil around roast, and place it in the air fryer.
- Now, pour gravy on top and then place butter on it.
- Air fry for 30–45 minutes until beef is cooked inside.
- Once done, serve with gravy and season with parsley.

12. CRISPY LAMB

SERVINGS: 8; PREP TIME: 10 MINUTES; COOKING TIME: 30 MINUTES
NUTRITIONAL VALUE PER SERVING: 230 KCAL; CARBS: 10G; PROTEIN: 12G; FAT: 2G

INGREDIENTS:

- 3 medium-sized eggs
- 1 garlic clove
- 20g breadcrumbs
- 2 tbsp. olive oil
- 2 bunches rosemary, chopped
- 30g macadamia nuts
- 1.6 kg rack of lamb
- A pinch of salt and black pepper

INSTRUCTIONS:

- Mix oil with garlic and stir well. Season lamb with salt and pepper and brush with oil.
- In another bowl, mix macadamia nuts with rosemary and breadcrumbs.
- Put eggs in a separate bowl and whisk well.
- Dip lamb in egg and then the macadamia sauce, and place it in your air fryer basket at 180°C for 25 minutes. Then, increase the temperature to 200°C for 5 minutes.
- Serve it.

13. LAMB AND AUBERGINE MEATLOAF

SERVINGS: 2; PREP TIME: 35 MINUTES; COOKING TIME: 5 MINUTES
NUTRITIONAL VALUE PER SERVING: 263 KCAL; CARBS: 6G; PROTEIN: 15G; FAT: 12G

INGRENKEDIENTS:

- A pinch of coriander powder
- 15g white onion
- 1 small egg
- 1 aubergine
- 1 kg stew meat
- 1 tbsp. fresh coriander
- 1 tbsp. tomato paste
- Cooking spray
- A pinch of salt and black pepper

INSTRUCTIONS:

- In a bowl, mix diced aubergine with lamb and the other ingredients, except for cooking spray.
- Grease a meatloaf pan and add the lamb to it.
- Put the pan in an air fryer at 190°C for 35 minutes.
- Slice and serve with salad.

14. LAMB AND SPINACH MIX

SERVINGS: 2; PREP TIME: 35 MINUTES; COOKING TIME: 10 MINUTES
NUTRITIONAL VALUE PER SERVING: 160 KCAL; CARBS: 17G; PROTEIN: 20G; FAT: 6G

INGREDIENTS:

- 225g lamb
- 225g spinach
- 15g red onion
- 175g fresh tomatoes
- A pinch of garam masala
- A pinch of chilli powder
- A pinch of turmeric
- A pinch of garlic powder
- A pinch of ginger powder
- A pinch of cardamom powder
- A pinch of coriander powder
- A pinch of cumin powder

INSTRUCTIONS:

- Preheat the air fryer to 180°C.
- Mix lamb with spinach, chopped tomatoes, diced onion, and spices.
- Put the mixture in an air fryer and air fry at 180°C for 35 minutes.
- Serve it.

15. LAMB RACKS AND FENNEL MIX

SERVINGS: 8; PREP TIME: 10 MINUTES; COOKING TIME: 16 MINUTES
NUTRITIONAL VALUE PER SERVING: 240 KCAL; CARBS: 15G; PROTEIN: 12G; FAT: 9G

INGRENKEDIENTS:

- 20g brown sugar
- 60 ml apple cider vinegar
- 700g lamb racks
- 60g fennel bulb
- 60 ml olive oil
- 120g figs
- A pinch of salt and black pepper

INSTRUCTIONS:

- Mix fennel with figs, vinegar, salt and pepper, and sugar in a bowl.
- Coat the lamb well with the mixture and transfer to a baking dish.
- Put in your air fryer at 175°C until cooked through.
- Serve it.

16. ROAST LAMB WITH ROSEMARY POTATOES

SERVINGS: 5; PREP TIME: 5 MINUTES; COOKING TIME: 1 HOUR
NUTRITION VALUE PER SERVING: 464 KCAL; CARBS: 1G; PROTEIN: 63G; FAT: 21G

INGREDIENTS:

- 1.9 kg lamb roast
- 375g potatoes
- 1 tsp. olive oil
- 1 tbsp. rosemary sprigs
- 1 tsp. thyme
- 1 tsp. mixed herb seasoning
- A pinch of salt and black pepper

INSTRUCTIONS:

- Place lamb in a dish and add salt, pepper, thyme, and mixed herb seasoning.
- Put it in an air fryer basket and roast for 30 minutes to a temperature of 160°C.
- In another bowl, add peeled potatoes, salt, pepper, rosemary, and olive oil in another bowl, and mix with your hands.
- When the lamb is roasted, add potatoes and roast for another 25 minutes.
- If the lamb still looks pinkish, roast for another 5 minutes.
- Serve and enjoy.

17. LOW-CARB CASSEROLE

SERVINGS: 4; PREP TIME: 20 MINUTES; COOKING TIME: 45 MINUTES
NUTRITIONAL VALUE PER SERVING: 182 KCAL; CARBS: 6G; PROTEIN: 17G; FAT: 12G

INGRENKEDIENTS:

- 1 tsp. fennel seeds
- 225g sausages
- 15g white onion
- 30g cheddar cheese
- Cooking spray
- 25g green bell pepper
- 4 medium-sized eggs
- 1 tsp. garlic salt

INSTRUCTIONS:

- Place sausages in an air fryer-safe pan.
- Add onion and vegetables, then cook at 200°C until the vegetables are soft and the sausage is cooked.
- Pour cheese onto the dish and cover it with eggs evenly.
- Add fennel seeds and garlic salt uniformly.
- Put the dish in an air fryer and roast at 200°C for 20 minutes.
- Serve it.

18. ROSEMARY GARLIC LAMB

SERVINGS: 2; PREP TIME: 10 MINUTES; COOKING TIME: 14 MINUTES
NUTRITIONAL VALUE PER SERVING: 427 KCAL; CARBS: 1G; PROTEIN: 31G; FAT: 34G

INGREDIENTS:

- 285g rack of lamb
- 1 tbsp. olive oil
- 1 tbsp. fresh rosemary sprigs
- 1 tsp. garlic powder
- A pinch of salt and black pepper

INSTRUCTIONS:

- Pat the lamb dry. Remove the skin if needed.
- In another bowl, combine rosemary, garlic, salt, and pepper.
- Add lamb and gently toss to coat. Cover and marinate for about 1 hour.
- Preheat the air fryer to 190°C. Spray the basket with oil and put lamb in it.
- Air fry at 190°C until lamb is cooked through.
- Serve and enjoy.

19. LAMB KOFTAS

SERVINGS: 4; PREP TIME: 10 MINUTES; COOKING TIME: 10 MINUTES
NUTRITIONAL VALUE PER SERVING: 450 KCAL; CARBS: 24G; PROTEIN: 33G; FAT: 22G

INGRENKEDIENTS:

- 110g ground lamb meat
- 1 tsp. coriander powder
- 1 tsp. garlic powder
- 20g white onion
- A pinch of salt and black pepper
- A pinch of cinnamon
- A pinch of turmeric powder
- A pinch of cumin powder
- 60g breadcrumbs

INSTRUCTIONS:

- Chop the onion finely. Add coriander, garlic, black pepper, and turmeric.
- Mix with hands to ensure a nice mixture.
- Make 4 koftas and put them onto a skewer.
- Preheat your air fryer to 180ºC. Put koftas in it, and air fry for 8–10 minutes until the lamb is cooked through.
- Serve and enjoy.

20. SPICY LAMB STEAKS

SERVINGS: 1; PREP TIME: 2 MINUTES; COOKING TIME: 8 MINUTES
NUTRITIONAL VALUE PER SERVING: 302 KCAL; CARBS: 0G; PROTEIN: 21G; FAT: 14G

INGREDIENTS:

- 140g lamb steak
- A pinch of salt and black pepper
- 1 tsp. chilli paprika
- Olive oil spray

INSTRUCTIONS:

- Remove steak from the refrigerator an hour before cooking and allow to reach room temperature.
- Preheat the air fryer to 200ºC, rub salt, black pepper, and chilli paprika into the steaks, and spray with a little oil.
- Air fry the lamb steaks until they are to your desired doneness.
- Cover it in foil for 5 minutes before serving.

Victoria Anderson

21. LAMB SIRLOIN FILLET

SERVINGS: 1; PREP TIME: 10 MINUTES; COOKING TIME: 15 MINUTES
NUTRITIONAL VALUE PER SERVING: 552 KCAL; CARBS: 36G; PROTEIN: 73G; FAT: 10G

INGRENKEDIENTS:

- 150g sirloin fillet
- 40 ml soy sauce
- 2 tbsp. oyster sauce
- 1 tsp. garlic powder
- 1 tsp. chilli sauce

INSTRUCTIONS:

- Put the fillet in a bowl and add soy, oyster, garlic, and chilli sauce.
- Rest the lamb for 1 hour.
- Preheat the air fryer to 185°C.
- Spray oil in the basket. Now put the lamb into it. Air fry until the lamb is cooked through.
- Serve with salad.

22. BUTTERFLIED ROAST LAMB

SERVINGS: 4; PREP TIME: 5 MINUTES; COOKING TIME: 30 MINUTES
NUTRITIONAL VALUE PER SERVING: 181 KCAL; CARBS: 1G; PROTEIN: 18G; FAT: 11G

INGREDIENTS:

- 600g butterflied lamb leg
- 2 tbsp. olive oil
- 2 tsp. rosemary sprigs
- 2 tsp. thyme
- 1 tsp. black pepper

INSTRUCTIONS:

- Preheat your air fryer to 180°C.
- Mix olive oil with rosemary and thyme. Rub this mixture into the lamb.
- Place lamb in air fryer for 18–20 minutes.
- Rest in foil for 5 minutes before serving.

23. BBQ PORK RIBS

SERVINGS: 6; PREP TIME: 5 HOURS; COOKING TIME: 25 MINUTES
NUTRITIONAL VALUE PER SERVING: 346 KCAL; CARB: 5G; PROTEIN: 22G; FAT: 11G

INGRENKEDIENTS:

- 900g pork ribs
- 60 ml maple syrup
- 2 tbsp. cayenne powder
- 1 tbsp. oregano
- 1 tbsp. sesame oil
- 1 tbsp. soy sauce
- 1 tbsp. garlic powder
- 100 ml BBQ sauce
- A pinch of salt and black pepper

INSTRUCTIONS:

- Combine all ingredients in a bowl (saving 1 tbsp. maple syrup for later) and leave to marinate for 5 hours or overnight.
- Preheat the air fryer to 200°C.
- Now put pork in the air fryer.
- Air fry for 15–20 minutes; flip, then brush with 1 tbsp. maple syrup.
- Serve and enjoy.

24. GARLIC LEMON PORK CHOPS

SERVINGS: 3; PREP TIME: 5 MINUTES; COOKING TIME: 50 MINUTES
NUTRITIONAL VALUE PER SERVING: 623 KCAL; CARBS: 1.3G; PROTEIN: 41G; FAT: 49.4G

INGREDIENTS:

- 1 tbsp. olive oil
- 1 tbsp. fresh parsley
- 900g pork chops
- 2 tbsp. lemon juice
- 2 tbsp. garlic powder
- A pinch of salt and pepper

INSTRUCTIONS:

- Mix olive oil, parsley, garlic, and lemon juice in a small bowl. Season pork chops with salt and pepper.
- Pour this mixture over pork chops, coating well.
- Add marinated chops into an air fryer basket and air fry at 200°C for 20 minutes.
- Serve and enjoy.

25. GLAZED PORK SHOULDER

SERVINGS: 2; PREP TIME: 15 MINUTES; COOKING TIME: 23 MINUTES
NUTRITIONAL VALUE PER SERVING: 475 KCAL; CARBS: 8G; PROTEIN: 36G; FAT: 32G

INGRENKEDIENTS:

- 2 tsp. honey
- 100 ml soy sauce
- 1 kg pork shoulder
- 2 tbsp. white sugar

INSTRUCTIONS:

- Mix soy sauce, sugar, and honey in a bowl. Coat the pork in this marinade and refrigerate for 6 hours (or overnight).
- Preheat the air fryer to 165°C.
- Grease a pan with oil and put the marinated pork in it.
- Air fry for about 20 minute or until cooked through.
- Before serving, wrap in aluminium foil for 5 minutes.

26. PORK TENDERLOIN

SERVINGS: 8; PREP TIME: 15 MINUTES; COOKING TIME: 30 MINUTES
NUTRITIONAL VALUE PER SERVING: 217 KCAL; CARBS: 1G; PROTEIN: 36G; FAT: 7G

INGREDIENTS:

- 1.4 kg pork tenderloin
- 2 tbsp. olive oil
- 1 tsp. garlic powder
- A pinch of salt and black pepper.

INSTRUCTIONS:

- Put tenderloin in the fridge for 20 minutes before cooking.
- In a small bowl, mix garlic, pepper, salt, and olive oil and stir well.
- Rub the mixture into the tenderloin and put it in the air fryer at 175°C for 10 minutes, frying until the meat is cooked through.
- Allow the pork to rest before serving.

27. PORK STEAKS WITH PICKLES AND CHEESE

SERVINGS: 8; PREP TIME: 10 MINUTES; COOKING TIME: 20 MINUTES
NUTRITIONAL VALUE PER SERVING: 270 KCAL; CARBS: 13G; PROTEIN: 20G; FAT: 7G

INGRENKEDIENTS:

- 2 tsp. basil
- 2 tsp. coriander powder
- 60 ml orange juice
- 1 tsp. orange zest
- 2 tsp. dried oregano
- 15g pickles
- 2 tsp. cumin
- 60 ml lemon juice
- 2 tsp. lime zest
- 1 tbsp. garlic powder
- 225g ham, sliced
- 225g pork steaks
- 340g Emmental cheese
- Olive oil spray

INSTRUCTIONS:

- Blend lime and orange zest with lime and orange juice. Add all the seasoning to it.
- Coat steak in salt and pepper and then toss in the juice and herb marinade.
- Put the steak into a basket and cover with the pickles, cheese, and ham.
- Air fry at 170°C for 20 minutes until roasted.
- Cut into pieces and serve with salad.

28. SPICY PORK CHOPS

SERVINGS: 2; PREP TIME: 5 MINUTES; COOKING TIME: 15 MINUTES
NUTRITIONAL VALUE: 305 KCAL; CARBS: 1G; PROTEIN: 35G; FAT: 16G

INGREDIENTS:

- 70g pork chops
- 30g Parmesan cheese
- 1 tsp. chilli paprika
- 1 tsp. garlic powder
- A pinch of salt and black pepper
- 1 tsp. parsley
- 1 tbsp. olive oil

INSTRUCTIONS:

- Preheat your air fryer to 190°C. Combine cheese, paprika, garlic powder, and salt in a dish.
- Coat each chop in olive oil and then coat each chop in the spicy cheese mixture.
- Cook in an air fryer for 10 minutes.
- Let it rest for 5 minutes, then serve.

29. PORK DUMPLINGS

SERVINGS: 3; PREP TIME: 30 MINUTES; COOKING TIME: 1 HOUR
NUTRITIONAL VALUE PER SERVING: 140 KCAL; CARBS: 16G; PROTEIN: 7G; FAT: 5G

INGRENKEDIENTS:

- 180g chopped bok choy
- 1 tsp. ginger powder
- 1 tsp. garlic powder
- 60g minced pork
- A pinch of crushed red chilli pepper
- 250g dumpling wrappers
- 1 tbsp. rice vinegar
- 1 tsp. soy sauce
- 1 tsp. sesame oil
- A sprinkle of brown sugar
- 2 tsp. chopped chives

INSTRUCTIONS:

- Heat oil in a skillet over medium-high. Add bok choy and stir while frying until wilted for 6–8 minutes.
- Add ginger and garlic and fry for 1 minute. Put in a tray and dry with a paper towel.
- Stir ground pork, bok choy, and red chilli pepper in a bowl.
- Put dumpling wraps on a surface and add one tablespoon, filling it in. With the help of a brush, moisten the edges.
- Coat the basket with cooking spray. Air fry dumplings at 190°C until golden brown.
- Stir rice vinegar, soy sauce, sesame oil, brown sugar, and chives in a bowl.
- Serve each dumpling with this sauce.

30. JERK PORK SKEWERS WITH BLACK BEAN MANGO SALSA

SERVINGS: 8; PREP TIME: 20 MINUTES; COOKING TIME: 35 MINUTES
NUTRITIONAL VALUE PER SERVING: 266 KCAL; CARBS: 23G; PROTEIN: 27G; FAT: 7G

INGREDIENTS:

- 60g desiccated coconut
- 2 tbsp. jerk seasoning
- 450g pork tenderloin
- 30 ml vegetable oil
- 1 mango
- 840g black beans
- 60 ml lime juice
- 2 tbsp. honey
- 2 tbsp. fresh coriander
- A pinch of salt and black pepper
- 60g white sugar
- 50g white onion
- 1 tsp. thyme
- 1 tbsp. cayenne powder
- 1 tbsp. nutmeg
- 1 tsp. cloves

INSTRUCTIONS:

- Soak a bamboo skewer in water for at least 30 minutes. Then, preheat the air fryer to 175°C.
- In a bowl, combine coconut, honey, and seasoning/spices. Coat the pork chunks in this marinade.
- Thread pork chunks onto skewers then brush with oil.
- Put skewers in an air fryer basket and air fry for 5 minutes until the pork is cooked through.
- In a bowl, chop and mash the mango.
- Serve the pork with mango, black beans, and fresh coriander.

31. HONEY-BAKED HAM

SERVINGS: 3; PREP TIME: 5 MINUTES; COOKING TIME: 45 MINUTES
NUTRITIONAL VALUE PER SERVING: 190 KCAL; CARBS: 8G; PROTEIN: 27G; FAT: 6G

INGRENKEDIENTS:

- 360g ham (pre-cooked)
- 90 ml water
- 1 tbsp. brown sugar
- 1 tbsp. honey
- 1 tbsp. Dijon mustard
- 1 tsp. pineapple juice
- A pinch of clove powder

INSTRUCTIONS:

- Preheat the air fryer to 150°C for 3 minutes. Put the ham in a small pan or baking dish, add water, and air fry for 15 minutes.

- Whisk brown sugar, honey, mustard, pineapple, and clove powder in a small bowl.

- Bake ham for another 15–20 minutes after glazing it with the homey mixture. Air fry until ham is caramelized.

- Remove from the air fryer and wrap in foil; let it rest for 5 minutes.

- Serve and enjoy.

POULTRY

Don't Forget To Get The Color Images FREE!
Simply Scan The QR Code Below!

Please scan the QR code below to access your bonus PDF with all 150 recipes with full coloured photos & beautiful designs alongside!

This is the only way we can get the recipes with coloured photos to you & keep the book as reasonably priced as possible.

Also, once downloaded you can take the PDF with you digitally wherever you go- meaning you can cook these recipes wherever you may be! (As long as you have an air fryer!)

We hope you enjoy and do let us know your feedback!

STEP BY STEP Guide To Access-

1. *Open Your Phones (Or Any Device You Want The Book On) Back Camera. The Back Camera Is The One You use as if you are taking a picture of someone.*

2. *Simply point your Camera at the QR code and 'tap' the QR code with your finger to focus the camera.*

3. *A link / pop up will appear. Simply tap that (and make sure you have internet connection) and the FREE PDF containing all of the coloured images should appear.*

4. *Now you have access to these FOREVER. Simply 'Bookmark' The tab it opened on, or download the document and take wherever you want.*

5. *Repeat this on any device you want it on! (If you want it on a laptop, simply email the document to yourself!)*

*Any issues please email us at **vicandersonpublishing@gmail.com** and we will be happy to help!!*

1. CHICKEN BREASTS WITH TOMATO SAUCE

SERVINGS: 8; PREP TIME: 10 MINUTES; COOKING TIME: 20 MINUTES
NUTRITIONAL VALUE PER SERVING: 260 KCAL; CARBS: 19G; PROTEIN: 28G; FAT: 14G

INGRENKEDIENTS:

- 225g chicken breast
- 120 ml balsamic vinegar
- 60g Parmesan cheese
- 1 tsp. garlic powder
- 30g red onion
- 600g canned tomatoes
- Cooking spray
- A pinch of salt and black pepper

INSTRUCTIONS:

- Preheat the air fryer at 180°C. Spray cooking oil in the basket of the air fryer.
- Add chicken and season with salt, black pepper, balsamic vinegar, tomato, and cheese, coating well.
- Air fry until the chicken is cooked through.
- Put onto plates and serve.

2. CHICKEN PARMESAN

SERVINGS: 8; PREP TIME: 21 MINUTES; COOKING TIME: 9 MINUTES
NUTRITIONAL VALUE PER SERVING: 251 KCAL; CARBS: 14G; PROTEIN: 31G; FAT: 9.5G

INGREDIENTS:

- 400g chicken breast
- 80g breadcrumbs
- 2 tbsp. melted butter
- 300g marinara sauce
- Cooking spray
- 120g mozzarella cheese
- 30g Parmesan cheese

INSTRUCTIONS:

- Preheat the air fryer to 180°C. Coat the air fryer with cooking spray.
- In a small bowl, combine breadcrumbs and Parmesan cheese.
- Brush melted butter on the chicken before dipping it in the breadcrumb mixture.
- Spray oil on chicken before putting it in the air fryer and air fry until cooked through.
- Top it with marinara sauce and mozzarella and air fry for another 3 minutes.
- Serve and enjoy.

3. FRIED CHICKEN TENDERLOIN

SERVING: 8; PREP TIME: 10 MINUTES; COOKING TIME: 15 MINUTES
NUTRITIONAL VALUE: 307 KCAL; CARBS: 3G; PROTEIN: 32G; FAT: 18G

INGRENKEDIENTS:

- 450g chicken tenderloins
- 150g almond flour
- 3 medium-sized eggs
- 60 ml oil
- A pinch of salt and pepper

INSTRUCTIONS:

- Preheat the air fryer at 195°C. Season chicken with salt and pepper.
- Soak chicken in beaten egg then dip in almond flour.
- Spray with cooking oil and air fry for 15 minutes at 195°C.
- Shake the basket halfway to air fry evenly.
- Serve and enjoy.

4. SESAME CHICKEN

SERVINGS: 2; PREP TIME: 20 MINUTES; COOKING TIME: 15 MINUTES
NUTRITIONAL VALUE PER SERVING: 302 KCAL; CARBS: 18G; PROTEIN: 26G; FAT: 13G

INGREDIENTS:

- 25g corn flour
- 1 tsp. soy sauce
- A sprinkle of sesame seeds
- 1 tbsp. chopped chives
- 225g chicken thighs
- 1 medium-sized egg
- A pinch of salt
- 50 ml chicken broth
- 1 tbsp. ketchup
- 1 tsp. rice vinegar
- 1 tsp. ginger powder
- 1 tbsp. garlic powder

INSTRUCTIONS:

- Beat the egg and pour it onto the chicken. Mix 20g corn flour with salt and pepper and sesame seeds. Add egg-coated chicken to the corn flour and stir well.
- Place chicken in an air fryer at 200°C, and air fry until cooked through.
- Whisk the remaining corn flour with broth, rice vinegar, ketchup, soy sauce, and herbs and spices.
- Serve with this sauce, and sprinkle with chopped chives.

5. CHICKEN THIGHS

SERVINGS: 2; PREP TIME: 10 MINUTES; COOKING TIME: 20 MINUTES
NUTRITIONAL VALUE PER SERVING: 321 KCAL; CARBS: 12G; PROTEIN: 36G; FAT: 8G

INGRENKEDIENTS:

- 1 tsp. sugar
- 1 tsp. white vinegar
- 2 tbsp. sherry wine
- 2 tbsp. soy sauce
- 3 kg chicken thighs
- 60 ml sesame oil
- 200g white onion
- A pinch of salt and black pepper

INSTRUCTIONS:

- Season chicken with salt and pepper, rub with sesame oil, and add to your air fryer, then air fry at 180°C until chicken is cooked through.
- Add diced onions, sherry wine, soy sauce, vinegar, and sugar to coat the chicken, and air fry for 10 minutes.
- Plate chicken and enjoy with your favourite sides or salad.

6. BUTTERMILK FRIED CHICKEN

SERVINGS: 2; PREP TIME: 15 MINUTES; COOKING TIME: 20 MINUTES
NUTRITIONAL VALUE PER SERVING: 335 KCAL; CARBS: 27G; PROTEIN: 24G; FAT: 14G

INGREDIENTS:

- 225g boneless chicken thighs
- 125 ml buttermilk
- 1 tsp. hot sauce
- 25g tapioca flour
- A pinch of garlic salt
- A pinch of salt and black pepper
- 1 small egg
- 70g plain flour
- 1 tbsp. brown sugar
- A pinch of paprika powder
- A pinch of onion powder
- A pinch of oregano

INSTRUCTIONS:

- Combine buttermilk and hot sauce in a dish.
- Combine tapioca flour, plain flour, garlic salt, salt and pepper, brown sugar, paprika, onion powder, and oregano in a bag to combine all ingredients.
- Beat egg in a bowl.
- Dip chicken thighs in buttermilk, egg, and flour mixture, in that order, and remove excess coating.
- Preheat your air fryer to 190°C and line it with parchment paper.
- Put chicken thighs in batches and fry for 20 minutes or until crispy.
- Serve and enjoy.

7. SPICY CHICKEN BREAST

SERVINGS: 4; PREP TIME: 10 MINUTES; COOKING TIME: 20 MINUTES
NUTRITIONAL VALUE PER SERVING: 432 KCAL; CARBS: 3G; PROTEIN: 79G; FAT: 10G

INGRENKEDIENTS:

- 700g breast, halved
- 1 ½ tbsp. paprika
- 1 tbsp. ground thyme
- 1 tbsp. cumin
- 1 tsp. cayenne powder
- 1 tsp. onion powder
- 1 tsp. black pepper
- 1 tsp. salt
- 1 tbsp. vegetable oil

INSTRUCTIONS:

- Combine all spices and oil in a bowl.
- Dip chicken in this spice mix and coat it evenly. Let it rest for 5 minutes.
- Preheat the air fryer to 180°C.
- Put chicken in an air fryer basket and air fry for 10 minutes.
- Flip and air fry for another 10 minutes.
- Serve and enjoy.

8. CHICKEN THIGH SCHNITZEL

SERVINGS: 8; PREP TIME: 15 MINUTES; COOKING TIME: 12 MINUTES
NUTRITIONAL VALUE PER SERVING: 293 KCAL; CARBS: 17G; PROTEIN: 24G; FAT: 14G

INGREDIENTS:

- 450g chicken thighs
- 120g breadcrumbs
- 1 tsp. salt
- 1 tsp. black pepper
- 70g plain flour
- 3 medium-sized eggs
- 1 tbsp. avocado oil

INSTRUCTIONS:

- Put chicken thighs on a sheet of parchment paper and flatten them with a mallet.
- Combine breadcrumbs, salt, and pepper in a bowl.
- Add flour in a separate bowl and beaten egg in another.
- Dip chicken in flour, egg, and then the breadcrumbs mixture, in that order.
- Preheat the air fryer to 190°C.
- Put chicken in the air fryer and air fry for 6 minutes, then flip and air fry for another 6 minutes. Check they are cooked through before serving. Cook for longer if needed.
- Serve and enjoy.

9. BBQ CHEDDAR STUFFED CHICKEN BREAST

SERVINGS: 4; PREP TIME: 10 MINUTES; COOKING TIME: 10 MINUTES
NUTRITIONAL VALUE: 379 KCAL; CARBS: 12G; PROTEIN: 39G; FAT: 19G

INGRENKEDIENTS:

- 170g bacon rashers
- 120g cheddar cheese, grated
- 60 ml BBQ sauce
- 225g chicken breast
- A pinch of salt and black pepper

INSTRUCTIONS:

- Preheat your air fryer to 190ºC.
- Air fry the bacon until crispy then cut into small pieces.
- Line the air fryer basket with parchment paper and increase the temperature to 200ºC.
- Combine bacon, cheddar cheese, and 1 tbsp. BBQ sauce in a bowl.
- Cut off the top of each chicken breast and create a small internal pouch.
- Stuff with the bacon/cheese mixture.
- Coat chicken breast with BBQ sauce and place it into an air fryer basket.
- Air fry for 10 minutes until meat is no longer pink in the centre.
- Serve and enjoy.

10. BUFFALO CHICKEN

SERVINGS: 2; PREP TIME: 20 MINUTES; COOKING TIME: 14 MINUTES
NUTRITIONAL VALUE PER SERVING: 234 KCAL; CARBS: 22G; PROTEIN: 31G; FAT: 5G

INGREDIENTS:

- 1 tbsp. Greek yoghurt
- 1 tbsp. egg substitute
- 1 tbsp. hot sauce
- 60g breadcrumbs
- 1 tsp. sweet paprika
- 1 tsp. garlic seasoning
- 1 tsp. cayenne pepper
- 225g chicken breast

INSTRUCTIONS:

- Whisk Greek yoghurt, egg substitute, and hot sauce in a bowl. Mix breadcrumbs, cayenne, garlic, and paprika in a separate bowl.
- Dip chicken into yoghurt mixture and then into breadcrumbs.
- Air fry for 14 minutes until cooked through.
- Serve and enjoy.

11. CRISPY HERBY NUGGETS

SERVINGS: 8; PREP TIME: 15 MINUTES; COOKING TIME: 12 MINUTES
NUTRITIONAL VALUE PER SERVING: 244 KCAL; CARBS: 24G; PROTEIN: 31G; FAT: 4G

INGRENKEDIENTS:

- 900g chicken nuggets
- 60 ml creamy herb salad dressing
- 60g plain flour
- 3 medium-sized eggs
- 240g breadcrumbs
- 1 tbsp. olive oil

INSTRUCTIONS:

- Put chicken in a bowl and coat with creamy herb sauce. Let it sit for 10 minutes.
- Put flour in a resealable bag; put egg and breadcrumbs in a separate bowl.
- Preheat the air fryer at 190°C.
- Place chicken into the flour bag and toss to coat, then dip the chicken into egg mixture, letting excess drip off.
- Spray a basket with oil and place chicken pieces inside the basket.
- Air fry for 6 minutes, flip, and air fry for another 6 minutes. Make sure that the chicken is cooked through before serving.
- Serve and enjoy.

12. HONEY CAJUN CHICKEN THIGHS

SERVINGS: 3; PREP TIME: 10 MINUTES; COOKING TIME: 15 MINUTES
NUTRITIONAL VALUE PER SERVING: 248 KCAL; CARBS: 16G; PROTEIN: 19G; FAT: 12G

INGREDIENTS:

- 60 ml buttermilk
- 1 tsp. hot sauce
- 340g chicken thigh boneless
- 1 tbsp. plain flour
- 1 tbsp. tapioca flour
- 1 tsp. Cajun seasoning
- A pinch of garlic salt
- A pinch of paprika
- A pinch of cayenne pepper
- 60 ml honey

INSTRUCTIONS:

- Combine buttermilk and hot sauce in a plastic bag. Add chicken thighs to it and let it marinate for 30 minutes.
- Combine plain flour, tapioca flour, Cajun seasoning, garlic salt, and paprika in a bowl. Now dip chicken in it.
- Preheat air fryer to 185°C. Put the chicken into the air fryer and air fry for about 15 minutes.
- Remove chicken from the air fryer and drizzle with honey.
- Serve and enjoy.

13. CORDON BLEU CHICKEN

SERVINGS: 2; PREP TIME: 30 MINUTES; COOKING TIME: 20 MINUTES
NUTRITIONAL VALUE PER SERVING: 427 KCAL; CABS: 20G; PROTEIN: 40G; FAT: 19G

INGRENKEDIENTS:

* 70g boneless chicken
* 30g deli ham
* 30g Emmental cheese
* 1 tbsp. plain flour
* A pinch of salt and black pepper
* 1 medium-sized egg
* 90g breadcrumbs

INSTRUCTIONS:

* Put chicken breast on a cutting board between parchments.
* Use a mallet to flatten it.
* Cut ham and cheese into four pieces. Put one piece of ham and cheese in the chicken. Roll up like a jelly roll. Secure them with a toothpick. Let it rest for 10 minutes
* Preheat an air fryer to 175°C.
* Combine flour, salt, and pepper in a bowl, beaten egg in the second bowl, and breadcrumbs in the third bowl.
* Dip chicken in flour mixture, egg, and then breadcrumbs to coat, in that order.
* Air fry the coated chicken for about 20 minutes until cooked through.
* Serve and enjoy.

14. CASSEROLE TURKEY WITH PEAS AND MUSHROOMS

SERVINGS: 2; PREP TIME: 10 MINUTES; COOKING TIME: 20 MINUTES
NUTRITIONAL VALUE PER SERVING: 271 KCAL; CARBS: 16G; PROTEIN: 7G; FAT: 9G

INGREDIENTS:

* 125g mushrooms
* 125g chicken stock
* 1 tbsp. celery, chopped
* 1 tbsp. white onion
* 35g fresh peas
* 500g turkey breasts
* A pinch of salt and black pepper

INSTRUCTIONS:

* Combine the turkey with salt, pepper, onion, stock, peas, mushrooms, and celery in a saucepan that suits your air fryer.
* Place pan in an air fryer at 180°C until cooked through.
* Divide between plates and serve evenly.

15. TURKEY FAJITAS

SERVINGS: 8; PREP TIME: 10 MINUTES; COOKING TIME: 13 MINUTES
NUTRITIONAL VALUE PER SERVING: 211 KCAL; CARBS: 16G; PROTEIN: 20G; FAT: 7.8G

INGRENKEDIENTS:

- 25g jalapeno peppers
- 25g bell peppers
- 50g white onion
- 60 ml lime juice
- 2 tsp. garlic powder
- 30g chili powder
- 900g turkey breasts
- 40 ml olive oil
- 1 tsp. onion powder
- 1 ½ tbsp. oregano
- 1 tsp. paprika
- 2 tbsp. fresh coriander

INSTRUCTIONS:

- Mix all spices, jalapeno, bell pepper, onion, and garlic powder in a bowl.
- Squeeze lime juice over turkey breasts, and sprinkle spices over them.
- Brush with oil and place aside.
- Preheat the air fryer to 190°C. Add turkey and air fry for 13 minutes until cooked through.
- Serve and enjoy.

16. TURKEY BURRITOS

SERVINGS: 4; PREP TIME: 12 MINUTES; COOKING TIME: 8 MINUTES
NUTRITIONAL VALUE PER SERVING: 349 KCAL; CARBS: 20G; PROTEIN: 21G; FAT: 23G

INGREDIENTS:

- 20g red bell pepper
- 60g avocado
- 30g mozzarella cheese, grated
- 4 medium-sized eggs
- 1 tbsp. parsley
- 670g turkey breast, pre-cooked
- A pinch of salt and black pepper
- 4 tortillas

INSTRUCTIONS:

- Whisk eggs with salt and pepper in a bowl. Pour into a saucepan and put in your air fryer basket.
- Air fry at 200°C for 5 minutes. Remove the saucepan from the fryer.
- Arrange tortillas and spread on the turkey meat, bell pepper, cheese, parsley, and avocado, and egg.
- Roll up and put in the air fryer for 5 minutes at 150°C.
- Serve and enjoy

Victoria Anderson

17. TURKEY LEGS

SERVINGS: 4; PREP TIME: 15 MINUTES; COOKING TIME: 30 MINUTES
NUTRITIONAL VALUE PER SERVING: 458 KCAL; CARBS: 2G; PROTEIN: 44G; FAT: 29G

INGRENKEDIENTS:

- 30 ml fresh lime juice
- 2 tbsp. fresh rosemary
- 2 tsp. lime zest
- 1 garlic clove
- 60 ml olive oil
- 1.8 kg turkey legs
- A pinch of salt and pepper

INSTRUCTIONS:

- Mix garlic, rosemary, lime zest, and lime juice in a bowl. Add turkey legs and gently coat them. Place this marinade in the refrigerator for 6–8 hours (or overnight).
- Set the air fryer temperature to 175ºC and grease the air fryer basket.
- Put the dish into the air fryer and air fry for about 30 minutes.
- Serve hot.

18. TURKEY MEATLOAF

SERVINGS: 2 PREP TIME: 20 MINUTES; COOKING TIME: 30 MINUTES
NUTRITIONAL VALUE PER SERVING: 435 KCAL; CARBS: 18G; PROTEIN: 42G; FAT: 23G

INGREDIENTS:

- 1 tbsp. breadcrumbs
- 1 tsp. dried oregano
- 1 tsp. cumin
- 60g green chilies
- 35g kale leave
- 60g cheddar cheese, grated
- 25g chopped onion
- 1 small egg
- 225g turkey mince
- 1 tsp. chilli powder
- 2 tbsp. fresh coriander
- A pinch of salt and black pepper

INSTRUCTIONS:

- In a bowl, add all ingredients and mix evenly. Divide this mixture into two equal-sizes and shape them into loaves.
- Set the temperature of the air fryer to 200ºC. Arrange loaves into the air fryer basket.
- Air fry for about 20 minutes.
- Remove it from the air fryer and put it aside for 10 minutes before serving.

19. TURKEY WITH GRAVYS

SERVINGS: 6; PREP TIME: 10 MINUTES; COOKING TIME: 3 HOURS, 30 MINUTES
NUTRITIONAL VALUE PER SERVING: 669 KCAL; CARBS: 6G; PROTEIN: 91G; FAT: 29G

INGRENKEDIENTS:

- 4 kg turkey breast
- 45g butter
- 1 tbsp. garlic powder
- 1 tsp. salt
- A pinch of black pepper
- 1 tsp. olive oil
- 80 ml chicken broth

INSTRUCTIONS:

- Completely thaw the turkey in the inside cavity. Tuck garlic and butter slice in between skin and turkey breasts. Rub oil in and season with salt and black pepper.
- Place turkey in the air fryer and spray with oil. Pour 40 ml of broth over the turkey.
- Air fry at 175°C for about 2 to 3 hours.
- After 30 minutes, baste with 40 ml chicken broth.
- Air fry until temperature reaches 73°C inside the turkey meat.
- Allow it to rest for about 15–20 minutes.
- Serve the turkey with trimmings of your choice.

20. STUFFED COURGETTE BOATS WITH SAUSAGE

SERVINGS: 2; PREP TIME: 10 MINUTES; COOKING TIME: 14 MINUTES
NUTRITIONAL VALUE PER SERVING: 285 KCAL; CARBS: 9G; PROTEIN: 16G; FAT: 21G

INGREDIENTS:

- 200g courgettes
- 110g sausage meat
- 30g breadcrumbs
- 30g grated cheddar cheese
- 1 tbsp. fresh parsley

INSTRUCTIONS:

- Halve and core the courgettes. Spray on the skin side with oil.
- Flip courgettes, stuff the centre with sausage, top with breadcrumbs and cheese, and spray with oil.
- Put courgettes in an air fryer and air fry at 180°C for 10–14 minutes or until sausage is cooked.
- Add fresh parsley and serve.

FISH AND SEAFOOD

Don't Forget To Get The Color Images FREE!
Simply Scan The QR Code Below!

Please scan the QR code below to access your bonus PDF with all 150 recipes with full coloured photos & beautiful designs alongside!

This is the only way we can get the recipes with coloured photos to you & keep the book as reasonably priced as possible.

Also, once downloaded you can take the PDF with you digitally wherever you go- meaning you can cook these recipes wherever you may be! (As long as you have an air fryer!)

We hope you enjoy and do let us know your feedback!

STEP BY STEP Guide To Access-

1. Open Your Phones (Or Any Device You Want The Book On) Back Camera. The Back Camera Is The One You use as if you are taking a picture of someone.

2. Simply point your Camera at the QR code and 'tap' the QR code with your finger to focus the camera.

3. A link / pop up will appear. Simply tap that (and make sure you have internet connection) and the FREE PDF containing all of the coloured images should appear.

4. Now you have access to these FOREVER. Simply 'Bookmark' The tab it opened on, or download the document and take wherever you want.

5. Repeat this on any device you want it on! (If you want it on a laptop, simply email the document to yourself!)

Any issues please email us at **vicandersonpublishing@gmail.com** and we will be happy to help!!

1. FRIED CATFISH

SERVINGS: 2 PREP TIME: 10 MINUTES; COOKING TIME: 13 MINUTES
NUTRITIONAL VALUE PER SERVING: 294 KCAL; CARBS: 26G; PROTEIN: 28; FAT: 18G

INGRENKEDIENTS:

- 1 ½ tbsp. fish seasoning
- 1 tsp. olive oil
- 75g catfish fillets

INSTRUCTIONS:

- Set the temperature of the air fryer to 200°C. Grease the pan with olive oil.
- Add seasoning to the catfish fillets, and toss to coat well. Drizzle olive oil on catfish.
- Put the catfish fillets in an air fryer basket and air fry for 10 minutes. Flip to the other side and spray with cooking oil. Air fry for about 3 minutes.
- Remove from the air fryer and transfer it to your serving plates.

2. FRIED CALAMARI

SERVINGS: 8; PREP TIME: 15 MINUTES; COOKING TIME: 10 MINUTES
NUTRITIONAL VALUE PER SERVING: 310 KCAL; CARBS: 2G; PROTEIN: 7G; FAT: 21G

INGREDIENTS:

- 900g calamari rings
- 300g breadcrumbs
- 150g plain flour
- 3 medium-sized egg
- 120 ml milk
- 1 tsp. sea salt and black pepper
- Cooking oil spray

INSTRUCTIONS:

- Preheat the air fryer to 200°C. Add flour to a bowl. Whisk egg and milk in a second bowl.
- Add salt, pepper, and breadcrumbs in a third bowl.
- Coat calamari rings first in flour, then in the egg mixture, and then the breadcrumbs mixture.
- Spray with cooking oil and put them in an air fryer basket.
- Air fry for 4 minutes; flip them, and air fry for another 3 minutes.
- Serve and enjoy.

3. CRAB CAKES

SERVINGS: 12; PREP TIME: 15 MINUTES; COOKING TIME: 10 MINUTES
NUTRITIONAL VALUE PER SERVING: 49 KCAL; CARBS: 2G; PROTEIN: 38G; FAT: 12G

INGRENKEDIENTS:

- 1 tsp. sweet pickle
- 1 tbsp. onion
- 65g reduced fat mayonnaise
- A pinch of salt
- 60g celery
- 1 egg white
- 35g breadcrumbs
- 40g crabmeat
- Cooking spray
- 1 tsp. celery salt

INSTRUCTIONS:

- Preheat the air fryer to 190°C. Mix egg white, pickles, onion, mayonnaise, salt, celery ribs, and a quarter of the breadcrumbs in a bowl and fold in crab gently.

- In a shallow bowl, add the remaining breadcrumbs. Drop a heaping mixture of crab in the breadcrumbs mixture. Coat the patties gently and form thick patties.

- Put crab cakes in an air fryer basket. Using cooking spray, spritz the crab cakes.

- Air fry for 8–10 minutes until golden brown; flip, and spritz with more cooking spray.

- Serve with your favourite dip and sides.

4. CREAMY TUNA CAKES

SERVINGS: 2; PREP TIME: 15 MINUTES; COOKING TIME: 15 MINUTES
NUTRITIONAL VALUE PER SERVING: 200 KCAL; CARBS 3G; PROTEIN: 23G; FAT: 10G

INGREDIENTS:

- 150g can of tuna
- 2 tsp. mayonnaise
- 1 tsp. almond flour
- 2 tsp. lime juice
- 2 tsp. dried dill
- 1 tsp. garlic powder
- A pinch of onion powder
- A pinch of salt and black pepper

INSTRUCTIONS:

- Mix in a large bowl the tuna, flour, lime juice, dill, mayonnaise, and spices.

- Make two patties from this mixture.

- Preheat the air fryer to 200°C.

- Arrange the patties in an air fryer basket and air fry it for about 10 minutes.

- Flip and air fry for another 4 minutes.

- Remove from the air fryer; transfer to plates and serve hot.

5. CRISPY COD STICKS

SERVINGS: 4; PREP TIME: 20 MINUTES; COOKING TIME: 7 MINUTES
NUTRITIONAL VALUE PER SERVING: 483 KCAL; CARBS: 38G; PROTEIN: 55G; FAT: 11G

INGRENKEDIENTS:

- 220g plain flour
- 30g green chillies
- 1 garlic clove, crushed
- 1 tsp. soy sauce
- 225g skinless cod fillets
- A pinch of salt and black pepper
- 3 medium-sized eggs

INSTRUCTIONS:

- Add the flour in a bowl, and mix in the eggs, garlic, chillies, soy sauce, salt, and black pepper.
- Coat the cod fillets in flour and then the egg mixture.
- Preheat the air fryer temperature to 190°C. Grease the air fryer basket and air fry for 7 minutes.
- Remove cod from the air fryer and serve warm.

6. SESAME SEED COATED HADDOCK

SERVINGS: 8; PREP TIME: 15 MINUTES; COOKING TIME: 14 MINUTES
NUTRITIONAL VALUE PER SERVING: 287 KCAL; CARBS: 20G; PROTEIN 9G; FAT: 18G

INGREDIENTS:

- 120g breadcrumbs
- 2 tbsp. sesame seeds
- A pinch of crushed rosemary
- 3 medium-sized eggs
- 90 ml olive oil
- 225g haddock fillets
- 80g plain flour
- A pinch of salt and black pepper

INSTRUCTIONS:

- Put the flour in a bowl, and whisk the eggs in another bowl.
- Add sesame seeds, breadcrumbs, rosemary, salt, black pepper, and oil until a crumb mixture forms.
- Coat each fillet with flour, dip in beaten eggs, then coat with breadcrumbs.
- Preheat the air fryer to 200°C. Air fry for about 7 minutes. Flip and air fry for another 7 minutes.
- Serve hot.

7. FISH TACOS

SERVINGS: 4; PREP TIME: 30 MINUTES; COOKING TIME: 10 MINUTES
NUTRITIONAL VALUE PER SERVING: 178 KCAL; CARBS: 22G PROTEIN: 16G; FAT: 3G

INGRENKEDIENTS:

- 50g reduced-fat sour cream
- 60g green chilies
- 1 tsp. coriander leaves
- 1 tsp. lime juice
- 110g tilapia fillets
- 30g plain flour
- 1 small egg
- 30g breadcrumbs
- Cooking spray
- A pinch of salt
- A pinch of cayenne powder
- 4 tortillas
- 40g fresh tomatoes

INSTRUCTIONS:

- Put reduced-fat sour cream, chilies, coriander, and lime juice in a food processor and process until blended, then set aside.
- Cut each tilapia fillet lengthwise into two portions.
- Put the egg, flour, and the breadcrumbs in three separate bowls. Dip tilapia in egg, flour, then in breadcrumbs.
- Preheat to 200°C. Air fry until fish flakes easily with a fork, 10–around 12 minutes.
- Combine seasoning, sprinkle over fish, and place a portion of each fish in a tortilla; top with 2 tbsp. cream mixture.
- Sprinkle with fresh chopped tomato.
- Serve and enjoy.

8. SOLE AND CAULIFLOWER FRITTERS

SERVINGS: 4; PREP TIME: 5 MINUTES; COOKING TIME: 24 MINUTES
NUTRITIONAL VALUE PER SERVING: 139 KCAL; CARBS: 14G; PROTEIN: 12G; FAT: 10G

INGREDIENTS:

- 455g sole fillets
- 455g mashed cauliflower
- 120g red onion
- 45g bell pepper
- 3 medium-sized eggs
- 1 garlic clove
- 60g fresh parsley
- 2 tbsp. olive oil
- A pinch of chilli flakes
- 1 tsp. paprika
- A pinch of salt and pepper
- Cooking spray

INSTRUCTIONS:

- Grease the basket with cooking spray. Put sole fillets in the basket.
- Set the air fryer temperature to 200°C for 10 minutes and flip the fillets halfway through.
- Transfer fillets into a large bowl and mash them into flakes.
- Mix the egg, cauliflower, onion, and spices together with the fish flakes.
- Make fritters: take two spoonfuls of fish mixture and mould into a patty shape.
- Air fry this for about 14 minutes.
- Remove from the basket and cool for 5 minutes.
- Serve and enjoy.

Victoria Anderson

9. THAI SHRIMP SALAD

SERVINGS: 4; PREP TIME: 10 MINUTES; COOKING TIME: 10 MINUTES
NUTRITIONAL VALUE PER SERVING: 209 KCAL; CARBS: 11G; PROTEIN: 23G; FAT: 9G

INGRENKEDIENTS:

- 70g shrimps
- 225g minced pork
- 2 tbsp. fresh coriander
- 90g spring onion
- 45g white onion
- A pinch of chilli flakes
- 2 tbsp. fish sauce
- 2 tbsp. lime juice
- 1 tsp. white sugar

INSTRUCTIONS:

- Put the onions in an air fryer pan and cook at 160°C. Add shrimp and let them fry on one side without browning.
- Once one side begins to be opaque, flip them over until both sides are opaque.
- Remove shrimp from pan and set aside cool.
- In the same pan, add minced pork and stir every so often until cooked.
- Don't allow the meat to go brown; reserve pork and juices on a plate and set them aside to cool.
- Then add the shrimp, pork, and the cooked onion mixture in a bowl.
- Combine fish sauce, lime, coriander, and sugar.
- Stir until sugar dissolves completely.
- Serve immediately with jasmine Thai rice.

10. BREADED SEA SCALLOPS

SERVINGS: 8; PREP TIME: 10 MINUTES; COOKING TIME: 5 MINUTES
NUTRITIONAL VALUE PER SERVING: 282 KCAL; CARBS: 14G; PROTEIN: 17G; FAT: 18G

INGREDIENTS:

- 120g butter crackers
- 1 tsp. garlic powder
- 1 tsp. seafood seasoning
- 60g butter
- 900g scallops
- Cooking spray

INSTRUCTIONS:

- Preheat your air fryer to 200°C. Mix cracker crumbs, seafood seasoning, and garlic powder in a bowl.
- Melt butter in a second bowl.
- Dip scallops in butter and roll in crumb mixture until completely coated.
- Set on a plate and repeat with the remaining scallops.
- Spray the basket with cooking oil. Air fry in an air fryer for 2 minutes.
- Turn scallops over gently with a spatula and air fry until opaque for about 2 minutes.
- Serve and enjoy.

11. LOBSTER TAILS WITH LEMON GARLIC BUTTER

SERVINGS: 4; PREP TIME: 10 MINUTES; COOKING TIME: 10 MINUTES
NUTRITIONAL VALUE PER SERVING: 313 KCAL; CARBS: 3G; PROTEIN: 18G; FAT: 26G

INGRENKEDIENTS:

- 460g lobster tails
- 120g butter
- 2 tsp. lemon zest
- 1 garlic clove
- A pinch of salt and black pepper
- 2 tsp. fresh coriander
- 1 lemon, cut in wedges

INSTRUCTIONS:

- Preheat the air fryer to 190°C. Butterfly lobster tails by cutting lengthwise through the centre of the hard top shell and meat with kitchen shears.
- Cut but not through the bottom of shells. Spread until halves part.
- Place tail in air fryer basket with lobster meat facing up. Melt butter in a small saucepan over medium heat.
- Add lemon zest and garlic for about 30 seconds.
- Put 2 tbsp. of butter mixture into a shallow bowl, brush onto lobster tails, and season it with salt and pepper.
- Air fry for 5–7 minutes until lobster meat is opaque.
- Spoon butter from the saucepan over lobster meat.
- Top with coriander and lemon wedges.
- Serve and enjoy.

12. SHRIMP AND POLENTA

SERVINGS: 4; PREP TIME: 15 MINUTES; COOKING TIME: 30 MINUTES
NUTRITIONAL VALUE PER SERVING: 331 KCAL; CARBS: 22G; PROTEIN: 22G; FAT: 18G

INGREDIENTS:

- 80g cooked polenta
- 60 ml olive oil
- 450g thawed frozen jumbo shrimp
- 100g fresh tomatoes
- 60g unsalted butter
- 1 tbsp. fresh parsley
- 2 tsp. hot pepper sauce

INSTRUCTIONS:

- Preheat the air fryer to 200°C. Lay polenta on a clean work surface. Cut into round slices.
- Brush both sides of slices with olive oil, and season with salt and pepper.
- Combine shrimp and tomatoes in a bowl.
- Add 1 tsp. oil and toss to coat.
- Air fry tomatoes in the air fryer for about 2 minutes until blistered. Then smash them with a spoon.
- Place shrimp in the air fryer and air fry for 10 minutes. Smash it with the tomatoes.
- Place polenta rounds in a basket and air fry for 15 minutes until they turn golden brown.
- Combine butter, parsley, and hot pepper sauce in a bowl.
- Put it on serving plates.
- Serve it with seasoned butter.

Victoria Anderson

13. CRAB RANGOON

SERVINGS: 12 DUMPLINGS; PREP TIME: 15 MINUTES; COOKING TIME: 10 MINUTES
NUTRITIONAL VALUE PER SERVING: 127 KCAL; CARBS: 11G; PROTEIN: 5G; FAT: 7G

INGRENKEDIENTS:

- 110g cream cheese
- 60g crab meat
- 1 tbsp. scallions
- 1 tsp. soy sauce
- 2 tsp. Worcestershire sauce
- 12 wonton wrappers
- 1 tbsp. sweet chilli sauce

INSTRUCTIONS:

- Combine cream cheese, scallions, soy sauce, and Worcestershire sauce in a bowl and combine evenly.
- Preheat the air fryer to 190°C. Spray the basket with cooking spray. Fill a bowl with warm water.
- Put wonton wrapper on a clean surface and add 1 tsp. of cream cheese mixture into the centre.
- Dip your finger into warm water and on the sides of each wonton paper. Crimp wrapper corners around upward to meet to form dumplings.
- Put it in the air fryer basket and spray it with cooking oil.
- Air fry dumplings for about 8–10 minutes.
- Serve sweet chilli sauce for dipping.

14. BANG BANG SHRIMP

SERVINGS: 2; PREP TIME: 15 MINUTES; COOKING TIME:12 MINUTES
NUTRITIONAL VALUE PER SERVING: 415 KCAL; CARBS: 33G; PROTEIN: 24G; FAT: 24G

INGREDIENTS:

- 1 tsp. Sriracha sauce
- 2 tbsp. mayonnaise
- 20g plain flour
- 65g breadcrumbs
- 225g shrimp
- A couple of lettuce leaves
- 2 tbsp. chopped chives

INSTRUCTIONS:

- Preheat the air fryer to 200°C. Mix mayonnaise, sweet chilli sauce, and Sriracha sauce in a bowl.
- Put flour on a plate and breadcrumbs on another plate.
- Coat shrimp with flour, then the mayonnaise mixture, and at the end in breadcrumbs.
- Put on a baking sheet in the air fryer basket.
- Air fry for 12 minutes.
- Serve it with lettuce; garnish with chives.

15. SALMON NUGGETS

SERVINGS: 8; PREP TIME: 20 MINUTES; COOKING TIME: 15 MINUTES
NUTRITIONAL VALUE PER SERVING: 364 KCAL; CARBS: 27G; PROTEIN: 26G; FAT: 16G

INGRENKEDIENTS:

- 160g maple syrup
- 1 tsp. smoked chilli pepper
- 1 tsp. salt
- 385g butter
- 60g garlic-flavoured croutons
- 3 medium-sized eggs
- 900g salmon fillet
- Cooking spray

INSTRUCTIONS:

- Combine maple syrup, chipotle pepper, and salt in a saucepan and bring it to a simmer over medium heat. Reduce heat lowly to keep warm.

- Place butter and garlic-flavoured croutons in a processor. Transfer to a shallow bowl. Whisk eggs in a separate bowl.

- Preheat the air fryer to 200°C.

- Sprinkle salmon with salt. Dip salmon in the egg mixture, then coat in crouton mixture. Then, you can put it on a plate and set it with cooking spray.

- Air fry for 3 minutes. Flip and air fry for another 3 minutes.

- Put it on a serving plate and drizzle it with the chipotle maple syrup.

- Serve and enjoy.

16. CRUSTED MAHI MAHI

SERVINGS: 2; PREP TIME: 5 MINUTES; COOKING TIME: 15 MINUTES
NUTRITIONAL VALUE PER SERVING: 304 KCAL; CARBS: 41G; PROTEIN: 27G; FAT: 9G

INGREDIENTS:

- 225g Mahi Mahi fillets
- 2 tbsp. olive oil
- 480g breadcrumbs
- 1 tsp. garlic salt
- 1 tsp. herb seasoning
- 1 tsp. turmeric
- 1 tsp. ground black pepper
- 1 tsp. fresh coriander
- 2 tbsp. lemon juice

INSTRUCTIONS:

- Preheat the air fryer to 200°C. Put fillets on a plate and drizzle with oil.

- Mix all seasoning and put in a shallow dish.

- Dip each fillet in the breadcrumb mixture and then the seasoning, and put in an air fryer basket.

- Air fry for 12–15 minutes.

- Remove from the air fryer and garnish with coriander and lemon juice.

- Serve and enjoy.

Victoria Anderson

17. SURF AND TURF

SERVINGS: 8; PREP TIME: 20 MINUTES; COOKING TIME: 20 MINUTES
NUTRITIONAL VALUE PER SERVING: 505 KCAL; CARBS; 30G; PROTEIN: 29G; FAT: 31G

INGRENKEDIENTS:

- 450g baby red potatoes
- 120 ml water
- 8 Cajun style sausages
- 200g sweetcorn
- 250g white onion
- 120ml olive oil
- 90g seafood seasoning
- 450g shrimp
- 1 lemon, cut in wedges

INSTRUCTIONS:

- Preheat the air fryer to 200°C. Place potatoes in a bowl, add water, and microwave for 5 minutes.
- Run bowl under cool water until potatoes are cool enough to touch.
- Slice potatoes lengthwise in a large bowl. Add sausage, corn, and onion. Mix in 6 tbsp. olive oil and 4 tbsp. food seasoning.
- Put shrimp in a separate bowl and add the remaining seasoning.
- Place half of the potato mixture in a basket and air fry for 10 minutes.
- Stir and air fry for 5 minutes.
- Add shrimp and air fry until potatoes are tender, sausage is thoroughly cooked, and shrimp are bright pink.
- Serve with lemon wedges.

18. MAHI MAHI WITH BROWN BUTTER

SERVINGS: 2; PREP TIME: 15 MINUTES; COOKING TIME: 20 MINUTES
NUTRITIONAL VALUE PER SERVING: 416 KCAL; CARBS: 0G; PROTEIN: 32G; FAT: 32G

INGREDIENTS:

- 170g Mahi Mahi fillets
- 75g butter
- A pinch of salt and black pepper
- Cooking spray

INSTRUCTIONS:

- Preheat the air fryer to 190°C. Season Mahi Mahi with salt and pepper. Spray with cooking oil on both sides.
- Air fry for about 12 minutes until the fish flakes easily with a fork and is golden.
- Melt butter in a small saucepan over medium heat; bring to a simmer until butter turns frothy and rich brown for 3 to 5 minutes.
- Remove from heat. Transfer fish to plates and drizzle it with butter.
- Serve and enjoy.

. 19. COCONUT SHRIMP
SERVINGS: 3; PREP TIME: 30 MINUTES; COOKING TIME: 15 MINUTES
NUTRITIONAL VALUE PER SERVING: 236 KCAL; CARBS: 28G; PROTEIN: 14G; FAT: 9G

INGRENKEDIENTS:

- 35g plain flour
- A pinch of salt and black pepper
- 1 medium-sized egg
- 30g unsweetened coconut flakes
- 20g breadcrumbs
- 170g shrimp
- Cooking spray
- 2 tbsp. honey
- 2 tbsp. lime juice
- A pinch of chilli flakes
- 1 tsp. fresh coriander

INSTRUCTIONS:

- Stir flour, salt, and pepper together in a shallow dish. Beat egg in another shallow dish. Stir coconut and breadcrumbs together in a third shallow dish.

- Dredge shrimp in flour mixture, dip in egg, and then in the coconut mixture, and spray with cooking oil.

- Preheat to 200°C. Place 1/3 shrimp in a fryer and air fry for about 8 minutes.

- Flip sides and continue to cook for about 4 minutes.

- Whisk honey, lime juice, and chilli in a bowl.

- Sprinkle with coriander and serve with the honey lime dip.

WRAPS AND SANDWICHES

Don't Forget To Get The Color Images FREE!
Simply Scan The QR Code Below!

Please scan the QR code below to access your bonus PDF with all 150 recipes with full coloured photos & beautiful designs alongside!

This is the only way we can get the recipes with coloured photos to you & keep the book as reasonably priced as possible.

Also, once downloaded you can take the PDF with you digitally wherever you go- meaning you can cook these recipes wherever you may be! (As long as you have an air fryer!)

We hope you enjoy and do let us know your feedback!

STEP BY STEP Guide To Access-

1. *Open Your Phones (Or Any Device You Want The Book On) Back Camera. The Back Camera Is The One You use as if you are taking a picture of someone.*

2. *Simply point your Camera at the QR code and 'tap' the QR code with your finger to focus the camera.*

3. *A link / pop up will appear. Simply tap that (and make sure you have internet connection) and the FREE PDF containing all of the coloured images should appear.*

4. *Now you have access to these FOREVER. Simply 'Bookmark' The tab it opened on, or download the document and take wherever you want.*

5. *Repeat this on any device you want it on! (If you want it on a laptop, simply email the document to yourself!)*

*Any issues please email us at **vicandersonpublishing@gmail.com** and we will be happy to help!!*

1. CHICKEN SNACK WRAPS

SERVINGS: 2; PREP TIME: 5 MINUTES; COOKING TIME: 12 MINUTES
NUTRITIONAL VALUE PER SERVING: 395 KCAL; CARBS: 36G; PROTEIN: 15G; FAT: 21G

INGRENKEDIENTS:

- 100g frozen breaded chicken strips
- 2 tortillas
- 30g lettuce, shredded
- 60g cheddar cheese, grated
- 2 tbsp. creamy herb dressing

INSTRUCTIONS:

- Spray the basket with cooking oil. Place chicken strips in a single layer and air fry at 195°C for 10 minutes.
- Flip chicken and air fry at 200°C for 2 minutes.
- Put the tortilla in the microwave for 20 seconds. Put cheddar and lettuce in the tortilla.
- Place chicken strips onto it and drizzle with creamy herb sauce.
- Serve and enjoy.

2. SUPREME CRUNCH WRAP

SERVINGS: 2; PREP TIME: 10 MINUTES; COOKING TIME: 17 MINUTES
NUTRITIONAL VALUE PER SERVING: 827 KCAL; CARBS: 39G; PROTEIN: 40G; FAT: 58G

INGREDIENTS:

- 2 tortillas
- 255g minced beef
- 40 ml water
- 1 tbsp. nacho seasoning
- 80 ml nacho cheese sauce
- 260g tostadas
- 80 ml sour cream
- 40g iceberg lettuce, shredded
- 40g fresh tomatoes

INSTRUCTIONS:

- Preheat the air fryer to 200°C. Cook beef in a large pan over medium heat.
- Drain fat and add 1/3 cup of water and taco seasoning; simmer it for 5 minutes.
- Cut tortillas and heat in microwave for 20 seconds.
- Put beef in the centre of each tortilla, and add cheese, tostada, sour cream, lettuce, and tomato.
- Brush with vegetable oil and place aside in basket.
- Air fry for 3–4 minutes until they turn golden brown. Flip and cook for 3–4 minutes.
- Serve and enjoy.

3. HOT HAM AND CHEESE WRAP

SERVINGS: 2; PREP TIME: 5 MINUTES; COOKING TIME: 10 MINUTES
NUTRITIONAL VALUE PER SERVING: 294 KCAL; CARBS: 17G; PROTEIN: 17G; FAT: 17G

INGRENKEDIENTS:

- 2 tortillas
- 110g smoked ham
- 1 tbsp. mayonnaise
- 1 tsp. Dijon mustard
- 1 tsp. butter
- 60g Emmental cheese, sliced

INSTRUCTIONS:

- Warm the tortillas in the microwave. Preheat the air fryer to 195°C.
- Spread a layer of mayonnaise and Dijon mustard onto the tortilla.
- Add ham and cheese slices.
- Brush it with melted butter. Cook for 5 minutes.
- Remove wraps from the air fryer and let them cool.
- Serve and enjoy.

4. HOT DOG WRAP

SERVINGS: 5; PREP TIME: 8 MINUTES; COOKING TIME: 10 MINUTES
NUTRITIONAL VALUE PER SERVING: 232 KCAL; CARBS: 10G; PROTEIN: 9G; FAT: 32G

INGREDIENTS:

- 225g hot dogs
- 190g bread
- 30g butter
- 140g American cheese

INSTRUCTIONS:

- Flatten each slice of bread with a rolling pin and set aside. Place American cheese in it.
- Place the hot dog on the edge of each slice of bread, and roll it with bread and cheese wrapping.
- Spread some butter on the exterior of the hot dogs.
- Air fry for 8–10 minutes at 200°C.
- Serve and enjoy.

Victoria Anderson

5. CRISP CHICKEN CAESAR WRAP

SERVINGS: 3; PREP TIME: 15 MINUTES; COOKING TIME: 11 MINUTES
NUTRITIONAL VALUE PER SERVING: 1,185 KCAL; CARBS: 152G; PROTEIN: 52G FAT: 42G

INGRENKEDIENTS:

- 75g chicken breast
- 3 medium-sized eggs
- 210g plain flour
- 80g corn flour
- 310g Caesar dressing
- 60g Parmesan cheese
- 45g all-purpose seasoning
- 30g croutons
- 25g lettuce
- 3 burrito tortillas

INSTRUCTIONS:

- Prepare chicken breast by cutting it into strips. Combine plain flour, corn flour, and seasoning.

- In another bowl, beat eggs until well combined. Dip chicken into the egg and then the flour.

- Air fry for 8 minutes at 190°C. Turn chicken strips and cook for another 3 minutes.

- Wash and chop the lettuce into strips. Add Caesar dressing, cheese, and croutons to a bowl.

- Spoon salad mixture and chicken strips on each tortilla. Roll in burrito style and serve.

6. TURKEY REUBEN WRAPS

SERVINGS: 4; PREP TIME: 10 MINUTES; COOKING TIME: 10 MINUTES
NUTRITIONAL VALUE PER SERVING: 278 KCAL; CARBS: 19G; PROTEIN: 11G; FAT: 17G

INGREDIENTS:

- 4 tortillas
- 90g sauerkraut
- 85g Emmental cheese
- 250g roasted turkey
- 10g butter
- A pinch of garlic powder

INSTRUCTIONS:

- Warm tortillas in the microwave for 25 seconds. Add one slice of cheese, 2 tbsp. of sauerkraut, and 2 slices of turkey.

- Tightly roll into burritos. Preheat air fryer to 190°C. Set the time for 5 minutes.

- Mix garlic powder with melted butter. Brush each wrap with garlic mixture.

- Air fry for 5 minutes until golden brown.

- Remove from the air fryer, cut in half, and enjoy.

7. BACON-WRAPPED TURKEY BREAST

SERVINGS: 8; PREP TIME: 15 MINUTES; COOKING TIME: 1 HOUR
NUTRITIONAL VALUE PER SERVING: 551 KCAL; CARBS: 3G; PROTEIN: 73G; FAT: 27G

INGRENKEDIENTS:

- 60 ml sugar
- 1 tsp. rosemary
- 2 kg boneless turkey
- A pinch of black pepper
- A pinch of paprika
- A pinch of clove powder
- A pinch of onion powder
- A pinch of garlic powder
- 60 ml oil
- 160g strips of bacon

INSTRUCTIONS:

- Preheat the air fryer to 180°C.
- Combine all seasonings and sugar and rub them on the turkey breast.
- Wrap bacon around the breast and make sure you cover it adequately.
- Air fry at 180°C until cooked through.
- Let it rest under foil for 15 minutes.
- Serve and enjoy.

8. HAM AND CHEESE MELT SANDWICH

SERVINGS: 2; PREP TIME: 5 MINUTES; COOKING TIME: 10 MINUTES
NUTRITIONAL VALUE PER SERVING: 455 KCAL; CARBS: 27G; PROTEIN: 21G; FAT: 29G

INGREDIENTS:

- 4 slices of bread
- 75g American melting cheese
- 115g ham
- 30 ml butter

INSTRUCTIONS:

- Lay bread, cheese, and ham; add another slice of cheese and then top with bread.
- Butter outside of the bread. Make sure to smear butter on both sides.
- Put sandwich in the air fryer basket.
- Air fryer at 180°C for 3–5 minutes to melt the cheese.
- Flip the side and increase heat to 190°C to increase the crispiness of the bread for 5 minutes.
- Serve and enjoy.

9. CRISP BUFFALO CHICKEN SANDWICH

SERVINGS: 4: PREP TIME: 10 MINUTES; COOKING TIME: 30 MINUTES
NUTRITIONAL VALUE PER SERVING: 290 KCAL; CARBS: 24G; PROTEIN: 28G; FAT: 7.7G

INGRENKEDIENTS:

- 455g boneless chicken
- 70g plain flour
- A pinch of garlic powder
- A pinch of paprika
- A pinch of salt and black pepper
- 3 medium-sized eggs
- 60g breadcrumbs
- 130 ml buffalo sauce
- 8 sliced of bread
- 1 tomato, sliced
- A couple of lettuce leaves

INSTRUCTIONS:

- Preheat the air fryer to 185°C. Combine flour in a bowl with all spices evenly.
- Whisk eggs in a bowl. Add breadcrumbs to another bowl.
- Dip a piece of chicken in flour mixture, then dip in the egg bowl, then dip in the breadcrumbs and press down until fully coated.
- Add chicken to the air fryer and bake for 15 minutes, until chicken is cooked through.
- Pour buffalo sauce on it.
- Toast a slice of bread and assemble the sandwich by adding lettuce, tomatoes, and chicken.
- Serve with your favourite salad, and enjoy.

10. CHICKEN FILLET SANDWICH

SERVING: 2; PREP TIME: 5 MINUTES; COOKING TIME: 25 MINUTES
NUTRITIONAL VALUE PER SERVING: 420 KCAL; CARBS: 39G; PROTEIN: 41G FAT: 10G

INGREDIENTS:

- 900g chicken
- 1 tsp. pickle juice
- 140g plain flour
- 1 tsp. garlic powder
- 1 tsp. paprika
- 1 tsp. basil
- 1 tsp. salt and black pepper
- 2 tbsp. peanut oil
- 240 ml milk
- 3 medium-sized eggs

INSTRUCTIONS:

- Cut chicken breast into pieces. Marinate chicken breasts in pickle juice for 1 hour.
- Whisk egg and milk together in one bowl. Place flour and spices in another bowl.
- Dip chicken in the egg mixture and then the flour mixture.
- Put in an air fryer at 190°C for 5 minutes.
- Spray with peanut oil.
- Air fry for 20 minutes.
- Serve and enjoy.

DESSERT

Don't Forget To Get The Color Images FREE!
Simply Scan The QR Code Below!

Please scan the QR code below to access your bonus PDF with all 150 recipes with full coloured photos & beautiful designs alongside!

This is the only way we can get the recipes with coloured photos to you & keep the book as reasonably priced as possible.

Also, once downloaded you can take the PDF with you digitally wherever you go- meaning you can cook these recipes wherever you may be! (As long as you have an air fryer!)

We hope you enjoy and do let us know your feedback!

STEP BY STEP Guide To Access-

1. *Open Your Phones (Or Any Device You Want The Book On) Back Camera. The Back Camera Is The One You use as if you are taking a picture of someone.*

2. *Simply point your Camera at the QR code and 'tap' the QR code with your finger to focus the camera.*

3. *A link / pop up will appear. Simply tap that (and make sure you have internet connection) and the FREE PDF containing all of the coloured images should appear.*

4. *Now you have access to these FOREVER. Simply 'Bookmark' The tab it opened on, or download the document and take wherever you want.*

5. *Repeat this on any device you want it on! (If you want it on a laptop, simply email the document to yourself!)*

*Any issues please email us at **vicandersonpublishing@gmail.com** and we will be happy to help!!*

1. COCONUT MACAROONS

SERVINGS: 18; PREP TIME: 15 MINUTES; COOKING TIME: 55 MINUTES
NUTRITIONAL VALUE PER SERVING: 103 KCAL; CARBS: 12G; PROTEIN: 1G; FAT: 6G

•

INGRENKEDIENTS:

- 200g sweetened flaked coconut
- 100 ml sweetened condensed milk
- 1 tsp. salt
- 4 drops of vanilla extract
- 1 egg white
- 85g bitter-sweet chocolate

INSTRUCTIONS:

- Preheat the air fryer to 160°C for 10 minutes. Cut a piece of baking paper to fit in the air fryer basket and leave 2 cm of space on each side.
- Mix coconut milk, salt, and condensed milk in a large bowl.
- Beat egg white in a bowl with a whisker, medium speed, until stiff peaks form about 90 seconds.
- Fold egg white into the coconut mixture.
- Transfer the coconut mixture to the air fryer basket, using a spoon to create 18 mounds of mixture on the baking paper.
- Bake for 9–10 minutes. Microwave chocolate for 30 seconds. Continue to microwave for 90 seconds until it is melted.
- Dip flat bottom macaroons into chocolate and shift to parchment paper until chocolate becomes firm.
- Serve and enjoy.

•

2. TRIPLE CHOCOLATE OATMEAL COOKIES

SERVINGS: 18; PREP TIME: 15 MINUTES; COOKING TIME: 12 MINUTES
NUTRITIONAL VALUE PER SERVING: 199 KCAL; CARBS: 25G; PROTEIN: 3G; FAT: 11G

INGREDIENTS:

- 120g quick-cooking oatmeal
- 100g plain flour
- 1 tbsp. cocoa powder
- 100g instant chocolate pudding mix
- A pinch of baking soda
- A pinch of salt
- 115g butter
- 65g brown sugar
- 65g white sugar
- 1 large egg
- 4 drops of vanilla extract
- 175g chocolate chips

INSTRUCTIONS:

- Preheat an air fryer to 175°C. Spray with cooking oil.
- Mix oatmeal, flour, cocoa powder, pudding, baking soda, and salt in a bowl.
- Mix cream butter and sugar in a bowl of an electric mixer. Add eggs and vanilla extract.
- Add oatmeal mixture and mix well.
- Drop dough into the air fryer basket using a large scoop into 18 mounds.
- Bake for 6–10 minutes until light brown. Cool on a wire rack before serving.

3. MINI SPONGES

SERVINGS: 12; PREP TIME: 10 MINUTES; COOKING TIME: 20 MINUTES
NUTRITIONAL VALUE PER SERVING: 88 KCAL; CARBS: 16G; PROTEIN: 2G; FAT: 2G

INGRENKEDIENTS:

- 140g plain flour
- 100g white sugar
- 60 ml water
- 3 medium-sized eggs
- Cooking spray
- 15 ml melted butter
- 1 tsp. baking powder
- 4 drops of vanilla extract
- A pinch of salt
- 60 ml confectioner sugar

INSTRUCTIONS:

- Preheat your air fryer to 190°C. Spray a 12-cup silicone mould with cooking spray.
- Whisk flour sugar, water, eggs, butter, baking powder, vanilla extract, and salt together in a bowl.
- Beat egg white in a bowl using an electric mixer until soft peaks form. Fold into batter.
- By using an ice cream scoop, place mixture in the silicone mould and cook for 10 minutes.
- Bake for 10 minutes and dust with confectioner sugar.
- Serve and enjoy.

4. BANANA CAKE

SERVINGS: 8; PREP TIME: 10 MINUTES; COOKING TIME: 30 MINUTES
NUTRITIONAL VALUE PER SERVING: 347 KCAL; CARBS: 57G; PROTEIN: 5G; FAT: 12G

INGREDIENTS:

- 135g brown sugar
- 100g butter
- 235g banana
- 1 large egg
- 60 ml honey
- 280g self-raising flour
- A pinch of cinnamon
- A pinch of salt

INSTRUCTIONS:

- Preheat the air fryer to 160°C. Spray a loaf pan with cooking spray.
- Beat sugar and butter in a bowl until it becomes creamy. Combine banana, egg, and honey in a separate bowl. Whisk banana mixture into a butter mixture until smooth.
- Sift flour, cinnamon, and salt into a combined banana mixture. Mix batter until it is smooth. Transfer it to a pan.
- Place the pan in the air fryer basket. Bake for 30 minutes.
- Check it with a toothpick to see if it is cooked throughout. If so, remove from the air fryer.
- Cool before serving.

Victoria Anderson

5. APPLE PIES

SERVINGS: 6; PREP TIME: 15 MINUTES; COOKING TIME: 10 MINUTES
NUTRITIONAL VALUE PER SERVING: 264 KCAL; CARBS: 35G; PROTEIN: 3G; FAT: 13G

INGRENKEDIENTS:

- 200g pie crust pastry
- 600g apple pie filling
- 1 small egg
- 1 tbsp. cinnamon sugar
- 1 tbsp. plain flour

INSTRUCTIONS:

- Put pastry onto a lightly floured surface and roll out the dough with a rolling pin.
- Use a 6-cm round biscuit or cookie cutter to cut the pie crust into 12 circles.
- Press 6 circles into 6 pie dishes or ramekins to create the base and side of the pie.
- Fill with apple pie filling. Do not overfill. Add the rest of the circles on top to seal the pies. Trim excess pastry if needed.
- Brush with beaten egg and sprinkle cinnamon sugar on top.
- Preheat your air fryer to 180°C.
- Bake for 7–10 minutes; serve warm or at room temperature.

6. BUTTER CAKE

SERVINGS: 4; PREP TIME: 10 MINUTES; COOKING TIME: 15 MINUTES
NUTRITIONAL VALUE PER SERVING: 470 KCAL; CARBS: 60G; PROTEIN: 8G; FAT: 22G

INGREDIENTS:

- 100g butter
- 75g white sugar
- 1 medium-sized egg
- 220g plain flour
- A pinch of salt
- 90 ml milk
- Cooking spray

INSTRUCTIONS:

- Preheat the air fryer to 175°C. Spray a small cake pan with cooking spray.
- Beat butter and sugar in a bowl using an electric mixer until it becomes light and creamy.
- Add egg and mix until it is smooth and fluff. Stir in the flour and salt. Then add the milk.
- Transfer the batter to the pan.
- Cook it in your air fryer basket for 15 minutes or until cooked through.
- Remove the pan for 5 minutes to allow it cool.
- Serve and enjoy.

7. FRESH CHERRY CRUMBLE

SERVINGS: 8; PREP TIME: 15 MINUTES; COOKING TIME: 40 MINUTES
NUTRITIONAL VALUE PER SERVING: 459 KCAL; CARBS: 76G; PROTEIN: 5G; FAT: 18G

INGRENKEDIENTS:

- 150g butter
- 280g pitted cherries
- 240g white sugar
- 2 tsp. lemon juice
- 280g plain flour
- 1 tbsp. vanilla powder
- 2 tsp. ground nutmeg
- 1 tsp. cinnamon

INSTRUCTIONS:

- Place cubed butter in the freezer for about 15 minutes.
- Preheat your air fryer to 160°C before you combine pitted cherries, 60g of sugar, and lemon juice in a bowl, and mix well.
- Pour the cherry mixture into a baking dish.
- Mix flour and 140g sugar in a bowl. Using your fingers, mix butter into the flour and sugar mixture. This must be crumbly rather than smooth. This is the crumble topping.
- Stir rest of the sugar, vanilla extract, and nutmeg in a bowl.
- Spoon the flour mixture on top of the cherry mixture, evenly.
- Dust sugar topping over the top of the dish.
- Bake in the air fryer for 25 minutes or until crumble topping turns brown.
- Leave crumble aside for 10 minutes to cool.
- Serve and enjoy.

8. DOUGHNUT STICKS

SERVINGS: 4; PREP TIME: 20 MINUTES; COOKING TIME: 5 MINUTES
NUTRITIONAL VALUE PER SERVING: 266 KCAL; CARBS: 38G; PROTEIN: 2G; FAT: 12G

INGREDIENTS:

- 115g ready-made bread dough
- 30g butter
- 50g white sugar
- A pinch of cinnamon
- 80g fruit jam

INSTRUCTIONS:

- Cut dough lengthwise. Dip these sticks into melted butter and put them in a single air fryer basket.
- Bake in an air fryer at 195°C for 4–5 minutes.
- Stir cinnamon and sugar together on a plate. Remove doughnut sticks from the air fryer and roll in the cinnamon sugar mixture.
- Serve it with jam.

Victoria Anderson

9. MINI NUTELLA TURNOVERS

SERVINGS: 6; PREP TIME: 10 MINUTES; COOKING TIME: 10 MINUTES
NUTRITIONAL VALUE PER SERVING: 163 KCAL; CARBS: 14G; PROTEIN: 3G; FAT: 11G

INGRENKEDIENTS:

- 25g frozen puff pastry
- 150g Nutella
- 1 tbsp. chopped hazelnuts, toasted
- 1 small egg
- 1 tsp. water
- 1 tbsp. plain flour

INSTRUCTIONS:

- Preheat your air fryer to 200°C. Place puff pastry on a lightly floured surface and cut with a sharp knife into 6 equal-sized rectangles.

- Place 1 tsp. of Nutella on one piece of pastry and sprinkle with hazelnuts. Fold the pastry over and press down the edges to seal. Repeat with the other pastry pieces

- Whisk egg and water in a small bowl. Brush egg wash over the edges.

- Air fry in the air fryer basket for 5–10 minutes.

- Serve and enjoy.

10. SHORTBREAD COOKIES

SERVINGS: 12; PREP TIME: 20 MINUTES; COOKING TIME: 3 MINUTES
NUTRITIONAL VALUE PER SERVING: 88 KCAL; CARBS: 12G; PROTEIN: 1G; FAT: 4G

INGREDIENTS:

- 100g plain flour
- 20g white sugar
- 60 ml butter
- 40 ml strawberry jam
- 40 ml lemon curd

INSTRUCTIONS:

- Combine flour and sugar in a bowl. Cut butter with pastry until the mixture becomes fine, crumbles, and starts to cling.

- Knead the mixture into a smooth ball.

- Preheat the air fryer to 175°C. Cut into shapes and sprinkle with sugar.

- Bake for 3 minutes until it turns brown.

- Serve cookies with strawberry jam and lemon curd.

11. CINNAMON TOAST

SERVINGS: 4; PREP TIME: 10 MINUTES; COOKING TIME: 10 MINUTES
NUTRITIONAL VALUE PER SERVING: 232 KCAL; CARBS: 22G; PROTEIN: 11G; FAT: 7G

INGRENKEDIENTS:

- 8 slices toasted bread
- 4 medium-sized eggs
- 120 ml milk
- 4 drops of vanilla extract
- 1 tsp. cinnamon

INSTRUCTIONS:

- Cut each slice of bread into three to make sticks, and place parchment paper in the air fryer basket.

- Preheat your air fryer to 180°C. Stir eggs, milk, vanilla extract, cinnamon, and nutmeg together until they are well mixed.

- Dip each piece of bread into the egg mixture.

- Air fry for 5 minutes and flip. Air fry for another 5 minutes

12. CHOCOLATE CHIP COOKIE BITES

SERVINGS: 8; PREP TIME: 10 MINUTES; COOKING TIME: 30 MINUTES
NUTRITIONAL VALUE PER SERVING: 188 KCAL; CARBS: 24G; PROTEIN: 2G; FAT: 10G

INGREDIENTS:

- 60 ml butter
- 50g brown sugar
- 25g white sugar
- A pinch of baking soda
- A pinch of salt
- 4 drops of vanilla extract
- 100g plain flour
- 80g semisweet chocolate chips
- 65g chopped pecans

INSTRUCTIONS:

- Put a piece of parchment paper in the air fryer basket. Beat butter in a large bowl with an electric mixer for 30 seconds.

- Add both sugars, baking soda, and salt to the butter and beat for 2 minutes.

- Beat in egg and vanilla extract until well combined. Add flour, chocolate chips, and pecans while beating.

- Drop 8 scoops of mixture on the parchment paper, set the air fryer to 150°C, and bake for 30 minutes or until golden brown.

13. APPLE CIDER DOUGHNUT BITES

SERVINGS: 20; PREP TIME: 10 MINUTES; COOKING TIME: 10 MINUTES
NUTRITIONAL VALUE PER SERVING: 132 KCAL; CARBS: 26G; PROTEIN: 2G; FAT: 3G

INGRENKEDIENTS:

- 315g plain flour
- 35g white sugar
- 1 tsp. baking powder
- 1 tsp. apple pie spice
- 1 tsp. salt
- 125g unsweetened apple sauce
- 115 ml sparkling apple cider
- 1 large egg
- 35g butter
- 1 tsp. apple cider vinegar
- 400g powdered sugar
- 4 drops of caramel extract

INSTRUCTIONS:

- Combine flour, salt, sugar, baking powder, apple sauce, and apple pie spice in a large bowl.
- Combine vinegar, egg, and melted butter in a bowl.
- Add wet ingredients to dry ingredients until just combined. Fill each silicone doughnut mould with batter, set the temperature to 175°C, and bake for 8 minutes.
- Cool for 30 minutes before glazing.
- Combine powdered sugar, sparkling apple cider, and caramel extract in a small bowl and whisk together until the glaze is smooth.
- Dip each doughnut in it.
- Serve and enjoy.

14. BLUEBERRY CRISP

SERVINGS: 4; PREP TIME: 10 MINUTES; COOKING TIME: 14 MINUTES
NUTRITIONAL VALUE PER SERVING: 217 KCAL; CARBS: 32G; PROTEIN: 2G; FAT: 10G

INGREDIENTS:

- 380g blueberries
- 25g plain flour
- 2 tsp. lemon juice
- A pinch of salt
- 55g quick cooking oats
- 20g plain flour
- 40g brown sugar
- 1 tsp. cinnamon
- 45g salted butter

INSTRUCTIONS:

- Preheat the air fryer to 180°C. Combine blueberries, flour, salt, and lemon juice in a bowl. Put in ramekins.
- Combine oats, flour, brown sugar, and cinnamon for topping in a small bowl. Mix in softened butter using a fork until the mixture becomes a crumb. Add topping to blueberry mixture.
- Place ramekins in an air fryer basket and air fry until blueberries are warmed throughout, and the topping is golden brown for 12–14 minutes.
- Serve and enjoy.

15. WALNUT PUMPKIN PIES

SERVINGS: 10; PREP TIME: 30 MINUTES; COOKING TIME: 7 MINUTES
NUTRITIONAL VALUE PER SERVING: 121 KCAL; CARBS: 14G; PROTEIN: 2G; FAT: 7G

INGRENKEDIENTS:

- 60g pumpkin puree
- 20g white sugar
- 1 tsp. walnuts
- A pinch of pumpkin pie spice
- A pinch of ground cinnamon
- 4 drops of vanilla extract
- 200g ready-made pie pastry
- 1 small egg
- 1 tsp. water
- 1 tsp. cinnamon sugar

INSTRUCTIONS:

- Whisk pumpkin puree, sugar, walnuts, pumpkin pie sauce, cinnamon, and vanilla until well mixed.

- Cut the pastry into 20 circle shapes, place 10 circles into ramekins or silicone moulds, and add the filling. Whisk egg and water in a small bowl. Add the top circles to the pies to seal in the filling. Trim around edge if needed. Brush the top of the pies with egg mixture.

- Preheat the air fryer to 182°C. Bake for about 7 minutes.

- Remove to cool down, then serve and enjoy.

16. CINNAMON BREAD TWISTS

SERVINGS: 3; PREP TIME: 15 MINUTES; COOKING TIME: 15 MINUTES
NUTRITIONAL VALUE PER SERVING: 105 KCAL; CARBS: 16G; PROTEIN: 5G; FAT: 2G

INGREDIENTS:

- 60g plain flour
- 1 tsp. baking powder
- A pinch of salt
- 75g Greek yogurt
- 1 tbsp. melted butter
- 1 tbsp. sugar
- 1 tsp. cinnamon

INSTRUCTIONS:

- Mix flour, baking powder, and salt before adding the Greek yoghurt. Use a fork to stir everything until crumbly dough begins to form. Leave some dry flour on the plate.

- Transfer the dough to a flat surface and make a smooth dough. Cut dough into 3 balls. Roll balls into long strips.

- Fold strips over and over to form twists and put them in the air fryer basket sprayed with oil.

- Air fry at 175°C for 15 minutes.

- Mix the sugar and cinnamon together.

- Brush cinnamon sugar and melted butter on top of the twists and serve warm.

17. CHEESECAKE CHIMICHANGAS

SERVINGS: 4; PREP TIME: 10 MINUTES; COOKING TIME: 10 MINUTES
NUTRITIONAL VALUE PER SERVING: 109 KCAL; CARBS: 10G; PROTEIN: 1G; FAT: 7G

INGRENKEDIENTS:

- 110g cream cheese
- 30g sour cream
- 4 drops of vanilla extract
- 30g strawberries
- 50g bananas
- 4 tortillas
- 25g Nutella
- Olive oil spray
- 1 tsp. cinnamon sugar

INSTRUCTIONS:

- In a mixing bowl, mix cream cheese, sour cream, sugar, and vanilla until smooth.
- Divide the mixture into a bowl and toss in the strawberries and bananas.
- Add the mixture and a dollop of Nutella into the middle of each tortilla. Roll up tortilla and spray lightly with oil.
- Preheat the air fryer to 185ºC. Bake for 8–10 minutes.
- When ready, roll each tortilla into a bowl of cinnamon sugar and serve.

18. STRAWBERRY POP TARTS

SERVINGS: 3; PREP TIME: 10 MINUTES; COOKING TIME: 12 MINUTES
NUTRITIONAL VALUE PER SERVING: 88 KCAL; CARBS: 88G; PROTEIN: 5G; FAT: 24G

INGREDIENTS:

- 170g ready-made shortcrust pastry
- 40g strawberry jam
- 240g powdered sugar
- 30g thick sour cream
- 1 tbsp. melted butter
- 4 drops of vanilla extract

INSTRUCTIONS:

- Cut dough into 6 rectangles. Add 1 tbsp. of strawberry jam to 3 rectangles. Add the remaining pastry rectangles as tops of the pop tarts.
- Use your finger to moisten the pie crust edge with water and seal firmly.
- Preheat the air fryer to 175ºC. Bake pop tarts in a basket for 12 minutes.
- Put pop tarts in the freezer for 10 minutes before frosting.
- In a small bowl, whisk powdered sugar, sour cream, butter, and vanilla extract.
- Spread frosting on top of pop tarts before serving.

19. BANANA PANCAKES

SERVINGS: 2; PREP TIME: 10 MINUTES; COOKING TIME: 20 MINUTES
NUTRITIONAL VALUE PER SERVING: 105 KCAL; CARBS: 20G; PROTEIN: 2G; FAT: 2G

INGRENKEDIENTS:

- 25g bananas
- 30g butter
- 30 g melted chocolate
- 420g plain flour
- A pinch baking powder
- 55g brown sugar
- 2 tsp. salt
- 165 ml milk
- 4 medium-sized eggs
- 240 ml sour cream
- 4 drops of vanilla extract

INSTRUCTIONS:

- In a bowl, whisk all dry ingredients.
- In another bowl, whisk milk, sour cream, eggs, and vanilla.
- Mix wet ingredients and dry ingredients.
- Line the air fryer basket with parchment paper and grease it with oil.
- Spread half the mixture on to the parchment paper thinly like a pancake should look like.
- Bake at 190°C for 17–20 minutes until it turns golden brown. Repeat with the rest of the mixture.
- Serve with melted chocolate dipping.

20. BROWNIES

SERVINGS: 8; PREP TIME: 10 MINUTES; COOKING TIME: 40 MINUTES
NUTRITIONAL VALUE PER SERVING: 315 KCAL; CARBS: 43G; PROTEIN: 4G; FAT: 16G

INGREDIENTS:

- 100g butter
- 250g bittersweet chocolate
- 3 medium-sized eggs
- 150g white sugar
- 2 tbsp. water
- 4 drops of vanilla extract
- 100g plain flour
- A pinch of baking soda
- A pinch of salt

INSTRUCTIONS:

- Preheat your air fryer to 160°C. Line the pan with parchment paper.
- In a clean bowl, microwave the chocolate chips. Cool slightly.
- In another bowl, beat sugar and eggs in water and vanilla. Mix flour, baking soda, and salt. Fold the chocolate mixture into the chocolate chips.
- Pour into a cake pan and bake for 40 minutes.
- When cooled, slice into 8 pieces. Enjoy.

Printed in Great Britain
by Amazon